GUERRILLA facebook MARKETING

GUERRILLA facebook MARKETING

25 Target Specific Weapons to Boost your Social Media Marketing

JAY CONRAD LEVINSON & KELVIN LIM K.M.

Guerilla Marketing Press
an imprint of
MORGAN JAMES PUBLISHING

GUERRILLA facebook MARKETING
25 Target Specific Weapons to Boost your Social Media Marketing

ISBN 978-1-61448-274-1 paperback
ISBN 978-1-61448-275-8 eBook
Library of Congress Control Number: 2012935464

Guerilla Marketing Press
an imprint of
Morgan James Publishing
The Entrepreneurial Publisher
5 Penn Plaza, 23rd Floor,
New York City, New York 10001
(212) 655-5470 office • (516) 908-4496 fax
www.MorganJamesPublishing.com

Cover Design by:
Rachel Lopez
www.r2cdesign.com

Interior Design by:
Bonnie Bushman
bonnie@caboodlegraphics.com

In an effort to support local communities, raise awareness and funds, Morgan James Publishing donates a percentage of all book sales for the life of each book to Habitat for Humanity Peninsula and Greater Williamsburg.

Get involved today, visit
www.MorganJamesBuilds.com.

This book is dedicated to all Guerrillas who run businesses in a tight economy. A Guerrilla will always be a Guerrilla, no matter where you are in the world, or the nature, or scale of your business.

TABLE OF CONTENTS

ACKNOWLEDGEMENTS

I would like to acknowledge co-author Shane Gibson of Vancouver, Canada, for ushering me into the world of Social Media with his landmark book, "Guerrilla Social Media Marketing." I also wish to acknowledge Kelvin Lim, for traveling halfway around the world to be a better guerrilla marketer, then giving wings to his potential with words and deeds.

—Jay Conrad Levinson

Every project involves the contributions of many "invisible" individuals, and this book project is no different. There are many people whom I am indebted to, and want to acknowledge.

My first thanks go out to Jay and Jeannie Levinson. It is a dream come true for me to work on a project with Jay together, an aspiration I've had since I was a college student. Jay, thank you for the opportunity to advance Guerrilla Marketing into print with me. You are my hero and an inspiration to everyone out there. Jeannie, thank you for being the most wonderful support and encouraging President of Guerrilla Marketing International for this project.

My thanks go out to my dearest friend Paul Ang, whose ideas and work match that of any true Guerrilla.

To my editor and partner-in-crime, Su-Ann Mae Phillips, it was fun spending all those hours ironing out this project. I look forward to many more opportunities with you.

To my team at Guerrilla Marketing Consulting:

I want to acknowledge Andre Lee and Stuart Tan, true guerrilla partners and directors of Guerrilla Marketing Consulting.

Eu Simin, for being a power-packed and most capable campaign manager that I know of.

To my team at Executive Coach International:

Thank you for your tireless support over the years. You have given me the space and resources I needed to work on amazing projects down various paths I have taken. I acknowledge all of you for your boldness and courage to live your lives to the fullest.

To my buddy Jimmy Wong, thanks for your friendship and partnership; may we have more exciting projects to work on together. You are one fine Guerrilla.

Finally and most of all, to my dad and mom. Dad, don't ever stop surprising me with your willingness and capability to move with the times. Mom, you are my inspiration and my reason. I love you both.

—Kelvin Lim

INTRODUCTION

Guerrilla Marketing and Facebook make great natural partners. They are both leaders: Guerrilla marketing is adopted and followed in many marketing strategies of businesses. No one can deny Facebook's presence. Facebook is irrefutably recognised as the leading social media tool, with some 955 million users.

They operate with the same principles: Guerrillas want the same thing everybody wants – but they don't have the same means, or they don't believe in excessive marketing budgets. So instead of splashing out on big budgets to net profits, Guerrillas' prime investments are time, energy, imagination and information. Facebook, like any other business, is driven to make profits. But they don't make their profits from getting people to sign up for Facebook accounts. Facebook's tagline sums it best: "It's Free and Will Always Be". Anybody and everybody above the age of 13 can sign up for a free, lifetime Facebook account.

They operate from the same premise: they recognize that their customers are active participants. The core of Facebook revolves around relationships. The basis of a Guerrilla Facebook

Marketing process is centred upon growing a relationship with the customer first.

Born out of this great natural partnership is our main reason why we are driven to write a book on Guerrilla Facebook Marketing, despite the fact that there have been precedents such as Guerrilla Social Media Marketing and Guerrilla Marketing on the Internet. There is just so much synergy between Facebook and Guerrilla Marketing that we find extremely hard to dismiss or ignore.

This book is the result of our journey of uncovering this great natural partnership between Facebook and Guerrilla Marketing. This book is going to stretch your mind with guerrilla marketing possibilities that any business can learn to adopt and apply. From Guerrilla basics such as attitudes and attitudes of a Guerrilla Facebook Marketer (Chapter 1) to Facebook basics such as Facebook trends and statistics (Chapter 2), to understanding the Rules of Engagement in Facebook for guerrillas (Chapter 3), we have the bases covered. We guerrillas always enter into battle with a plan, so we prepare for it by selecting weapons – in Chapter 4, there are 25 Facebook-specific weapons for you to choose from before you go on to create your Guerrilla Facebook Marketing plan and calendar in Chapter 5. After you have launched your plan, we take it a notch higher by suggesting ways to refine your plan by making sense of your investments in Chapter 6. By the time you are ready to fly into Chapter 7, we invite you to take your Guerrilla Facebook Marketing plan to the skies, by examining how your Guerrilla Facebook Marketing efforts faceoff with your online marketing efforts. The glossary on Facebook and Guerrilla Marketing concepts at the end of this book serves as a useful future reference point.

Even though this is a book, we see you, our reader, as an active participant in the book reading process. We have provided you with white space and exercises in this book for you to get actively involved in the reading process.

We wish you many happy hours connecting with your customers on Facebook that lead to profit generation for your business!

See you on Facebook.

Jay Levinson

CHAPTER 1

THE WORKINGS OF FACEBOOK MARKETING, GUERRILLA STYLE

Facebook, a modern social media tool like no other, has changed the way guerrillas launch online marketing campaigns today. It is free, accessible and easy-to-navigate, and it has levelled the playing field between the haves and the have-nots in terms of marketing budgets and resources. Facebook has helped many businesses generate market leads, build lists, expand customer base, increase sale conversions, and boost repeat customer sales.

However, Facebook has also been misunderstood by many. Many businesses are eager to join the bandwagon and connect with their fans, but without a deep understanding of how marketing works within the context of Facebook.

This is where we start. We put things in perspective by first highlighting the unique attributes and attitudes that could help you understand better how Guerrilla Facebook Marketing works. Facebook is a unique social media tool. It goes beyond the other social media tools, and offers great marketing potential for guerrillas. Appreciating its uniqueness can help us approach this amazing marketing medium better.

In this Chapter, we have identified ten such attributes of Facebook and ten attitudes of Guerrilla Facebook Marketers. Attributes are features or qualities that are regarded as characteristics of Facebook – you could call it an overview of Facebook culture from a guerrilla's point of view if you like. Attitudes are based on your beliefs – your ways of thinking that guerrilla marketers would want to emulate – you could call it guerrilla coping strategies for Facebook Marketing.

Attributes of Facebook

1. Authentic Conversations

Guerrillas value substance.

Facebook's platform was designed to help you generate authentic conversations. You can build trust, invest in communication, and pay regular attention to your customers through Facebook's many ways of communicating and interacting. This is the core of Facebook and this is how businesses connect their brands with their customers.

The web community is very discerning. This is a community that is not just interested in entertaining spectacles like flashy advertisements or clever copywriting. Facebook Marketing is your chance to expand the way the community see your business. You achieve this by letting them know who you are, and what your brand stands for. The beauty of Facebook and its community is that the community too wants to see if they can identify with your values and opinions. In other words, they are looking for authentic conversations with brands they feel connected with.

Customers today, more than ever, buy the promise of fulfilling hopes and dreams. They are not just buying a product or service, they are buying ambition, acceptance, beauty, confidence, convenience, comfort, friendship, gratification, health, independence, love, security, wealth, success... A brand, therefore, should also be treated as a promise. It is a promise that you, the business owner, make to your customers. And because your customers would buy based on your promise, you are obliged to uphold that promise with the respect it deserves. Businesses who understand this have harnessed the power of Facebook to reach out to their customers, and to build their brand reputation further and deeper with their customers.

This is the power of authentic conversations in Facebook.

2. Likeable Content

Guerrilla Marketing is based on the science of human psychology. There are two aspects that can make something likeable:

1. how something is expressed, and
2. how relevant and/or appealing the content is to the audience.

90% of purchasing decisions are guided by the unconscious mind. When a customer likes a brand, it is because the brand has consistently spoken in ways that appeals to the customer's unconscious mind. How you express yourself to your fans and customers is important. What do you want your Facebook Profile or Page to say about your business? Is your content compelling? Authentic? Genuine? Newsworthy? Delightful? Humorous? Provocative? Worth passing on?

Relevant and/or appealing content is also likeable. How do you create relevant and/or appealing content? Do you observe your fan's eyes, hearts and minds? What keeps them coming back to your Page for more? Do you know what they like about you (or your Page)? Do you know what interests them?

Whether it is humor, provocation or enticement, Guerrilla Facebook Marketers always aim to create high quality, likeable content. Creating likeable content is never easy to do, but it certainly goes a long way to get your fans to return for more.

3. Ongoing Attack

Guerrillas roll out their Facebook Marketing attack as an ongoing one.

We say ongoing – it is not just about being current or present. It is about keeping the attack going. A Guerrilla Facebook Marketing attack can be dynamic: there could drastic, tactical changes, there could be lull periods, and there could be periods of extreme activity… the bottomline is, the attack never stops. Guerrillas focus their resources on maintaining an ongoing attack. We are talking weeks, if not months, or years even.

Having a Facebook Page is not the same as having a corporate website. Your business' website would probably contain information that does not change over time – for instance, your background history, business philosophy, and to a lesser degree, your products or services.

Your Facebook presence, however, requires a totally different strategy. An ongoing attack is an intense one. Regularity breeds familiarity, and familiarity creates trust. Trust creates profitable sales from lifelong customers. For instance, your Facebook Page needs to be updated regularly. It doesn't make much sense if half of the 955 million Facebook users log in to Facebook every day, but you are only interested to connect with your fans once a month.

Guerrilla Facebook Marketing is not for everybody. It is hard work to maintain an ongoing attack at all times. It could cost you nothing to set up a Facebook page. But it will cost you some resources to maintain the Page on a regular basis. You will need resources to maintain an ongoing attack.

4. Real-Time Sensitivity

Facebook is about being present in real-time.

It focuses on being connected to those who are present with your Page in that moment. Over time, your fans would come and go, connecting with you at different times of the day, month or even year, but each time they do, they are connecting with you in real-time.

Guerrillas know that operating in a real-time environment means setting aside sufficient resources to engage in follow-up and being responsive in real-time to their fans. Take for instance, maintaining a Discussion Board on Facebook. Part of the real-time culture of the Facebook is the ubiquitous real-time stamp element of every status update, question or photo posed on your Page. Imagine: a sticky question is posed, and fans' comments are flooding in by the minute. What do you think are the implications of posting a response that is time-stamped six months later?

5. Millions of Daily Active Users

Guerrilla Marketers know that they are not the only show in town.

There are a lot of people connecting on Facebook each and every day – literally millions! This is the main draw why marketers are keen to jump on the Facebook bandwagon. It is irresistible for any marketer to ignore the attractiveness of having an audience this size. We guerrillas agree too. Facebook has the capacity to reach out to many. But this is where the misunderstandings arise. Yes, Facebook can connect you to millions, but no, this does not happen automatically – at least not without effort on your part.

Getting someone's attention on Facebook is much harder than you think. There is a lot of noise generated from other sources: friends, fans, businesses and of course, competitors. How do you stand out from the noise? What would make fans return to your Facebook Page, day after day?

Guerrillas also know that despite the numbers, connecting with fans is still very much a one-on-one game. Every customer is an individual, and every individual desires to be treated as unique when they log into Facebook. What will make your fans feel extra special?

6. Choice

Guerrillas want choice.

Choice enables flexibility. And Facebook offers it – plenty of choice and flexibility. Unlike the other social media tools such as blogs or YouTube that have a limited range of tools, Facebook has, by far, the widest range and depth of weapons and ammo for businesses to choose from.

This gives businesses the flexibility to choose whether they want to launch a targeted marketing attack based on specific demographics (e.g. age, gender, birthday, location, relationships or even interests), or whether they want to reach out to as many fans and visitors as possible within the shortest time frame on a global scale.

7. Data & Content Sharing

Guerrillas would happily leverage on someone else's data, as long as the job's done well.

On the surface, Facebook may be a social tool, but the real value guerrillas look for is what runs beneath. Every comment, sharing, upload and click on Facebook is traceable and monitored carefully. And the good news is, Facebook takes it upon themselves to carry out the gruelling work of data collection and processing. And that is not all. Facebook shares their data openly with businesses and marketers. The shared data is a treasure trove of information that is not limited to demographics, geography, friends, spending habits and Facebook activities...

Plus, there is more: not only is data access easy, data analysis is also made easy with the range of analytics offered by Facebook and third party vendors. No more muck or fuss to get the market research done.

Content sharing refers to user-generated content (UGC) that fans and visitors post to Pages. This is how fans interact with businesses to connect with them, sharing their stories, their opinions, their reviews, and so on. UGC provides guerrillas with another minefield of data for processing.

8. The Changing Face of Facebook

Guerrillas keep one eye open for what's next.

Facebook is constantly evolving. It is constantly changing its policies and the way things are done or presented. It is constantly working with developers to roll out new tools or features for businesses and users alike. Put another way, you could say that the business mode of Facebook is change and evolution.

Guerrillas know this. They prepare themselves for a steady slew of changes that would come their way while they navigate the Facebook landscape. But while guerrillas stay vigilant for what's next, they also approach change in moderation. They take time to sieve value from hype. When battling in the forest, they are aware of the danger of missing the forest for the trees by chasing down every other shiny new gadget or app that Facebook launches.

9. Social Enterprise

When there are hundreds – or thousands – of fans, Guerrillas ask, "so what now?"

You are running a business. You did not create your business Page as a purely social activity.

Who is buying what you are selling?

At the end of the day, having a strong fan base is not enough. There's still plenty of work to be done. It might cost basically nothing to set up a Facebook Page, but having a Facebook Page alone isn't going to magically ring in sales for your business. This is how business Pages in Facebook do not reach their full potential.

You still need to bridge the gap by converting your Facebook activities into solid action that would help you achieve your business goals. If it is to explore new markets, are you doing consistent recon to detect which combinations of weapons work for you? If it is to expand your online presence, are you monitoring to assess if your Facebook Page is generating traffic that leads to your business website and vice-versa? If it is sales conversions you want, do you have a battle plan to convert your fans into customers? If it is about sales generation, do you have a battle plan to get your fans to buy?

To lose track of the entrepreneurial aspect of this social tool, is to lose the war.

10. Facebook Connections

Guerrillas recognise the value of fraternizing with the enemy.

In business, what appears to be the enemy may not necessarily be so. If you change the way you view your competitors, your competitor could well turn out to be a co-operator instead. In recent times, Facebook has embraced this concept as part of their business strategy. As a whole, Facebook has been reaching out aggressively to the web community in general, offering links from external websites to Facebook Pages (and vice-versa), among other collaborations. As Facebook makes it easier for other online communities to interact with Facebook Pages and Profiles, we guerrillas are excited about the prospects of these connections. We can see how there's going to be plenty of positive side-effects, such as a boom in fusion marketing. To fuse is to focus on cooperation rather than competition. For example, while at the supermarket, you receive discount coupons for lunchtime specials to the diner next door.

While attributes are features or qualities that are regarded as characteristics of Facebook, attitudes can be viewed as winning strategies that guerrillas adopt to drive their marketing attacks. Here's our list of ten attitudes guerrilla Facebook marketers to be aware of:

Attitudes of Guerrilla Facebook Marketers

1. **Sincere.** Guerrillas know that to engage in authentic conversations is to be sincere about engaging and connecting with their customers. Although guerrillas measure success in terms of net profits, they generate those profits by deploying relationship-building strategies such as providing advice or helping to build trust with their Facebook Fans. Sincerity is an integral part of a guerrilla's Facebook marketing process. They genuinely want to know what their customers want in order to provide it for them. So they rely less on market research and more on personal contact they get on Facebook from their fans.

Without sincerity, guerrillas know that their emails will stink like spam.

2. **Creative.** Guerrillas need creativity to generate new content. From time to time, they could resort to rehashing content from elsewhere (such as from existing blogs or corporate websites), but from time to time, they will still need batches of fresh, creative and new content. They also need to be creative when it comes to managing negative feedback, or tackling new technologies and changes that would come their way in Facebook land.

3. **Patient.** Guerrillas are aware that customers desire relationships, but relationships do not happen overnight, and there is a need to keep the attack going. Plus, some customers have been stung before, and they don't want to be stung again. So it is going to take time to connect with their fans and visitors. How long? We say guerrillas need to give their Facebook marketing efforts at least two months to a year. Incidentally but definitely not coincidentally, patience is a time-honored guerrilla virtue.

4. **Relevant.** Guerrillas stay ahead of the game by keeping themselves updated on what their fans want. They tell their fans the kind of stories their fans want to hear, to keep them coming back for more. Guerrillas also keep up with changing technologies. The web is a place filled with opportunities for self-learning. If guerrillas don't know it, they learn it. This is how guerrillas stay relevant to the game.

5. **Dedicated.** Guerrillas stick to their plan and persevere. There's going to be plenty of distractions and they know it. If they are committed but lack dedication to see through the plan, they know it is not going to work. It's not just

going to take a while to build up a fan base; it is also going to be rough as they deal with negative comments, reviews, or bad press from their fans-turned-detractors.

6. **Respectful.** Guerrilla Marketers have long discerned that gone are the days of sales gimmicks, empty promises and cheesy ads. Guerrilla Marketing has an obligation to put money into your coffers, not just smiles - or looks of horror or shock or disgust - on the faces of your prospects. Facebook Fans are intelligent and discerning – they seek to be respected.

7. **Dependent.** Guerrillas are aware that it is a fool's errand to work alone. They know the outcome of their campaigns is strengthened by their collaborations with their fusion partners and suppliers, the commitment of their employees, and the loyalty of their customers. In other words, they are dependent on the community in which they operate in.

8. **Focused.** Guerrillas keep focused on delivering their marketing plan. Maintaining focus sounds easy but it is not easy to achieve in a cluttered world filled with many distractions. This is why they shy away from shiny distractions such as trying out every new gadget or app released on Facebook.

9. **Confident.** Guerrillas know they are the experts when it comes to their business. No one knows their business better than themselves, and when the moment is right, they are not afraid to show it, both on their Facebook Pages as well as on other online sites, such as forums or discussions.

10. **Direct.** Guerrillas strive to be straight up about who they are, and what their business is about. They are proud of their unique selling point. If they feel they cannot afford to be honest and direct, then they won't get involved in the

first place. They'd rather try other tools that could be more suited for them.

Now take a couple of minutes to consider how attributes of Facebook are linked to attitudes of guerrillas:

Table 1: Attributes & Attitudes

Attributes of Facebook	Attitudes of Guerrilla Facebook Marketers
1. Authentic Conversations	1. Sincere
2. Likeable Content	2. Creative
3. Ongoing Attack	3. Patient
4. Real-time Sensitivity	4. Relevant
5. Millions of Daily Active Users	5. Dedicated
6. Choice	6. Respectful
7. Data & Content Sharing	7. Dependent
8. The Changing Face of Facebook	8. Focused
9. Social Enterprise	9. Confident
10. Facebook Connections	10. Direct

Chapter 2

FACEBOOK RECON

Reconnaissance is at the center of a guerrilla's Facebook marketing strategy. The first step in a recon exercise is intelligence gathering: Facebook trends and statistics, user and usage patterns, and so on. Due to the huge interest in Facebook, it is not difficult to find useful and timely data. Facebook's official website offers a general summary, while there are specialized research groups that focus on Facebook data such as www.socialbakers.com and www.insidefacebook.com.

You know you need to know your enemy first. But how do you get started? To help you jumpstart your recon process, we have shared our list on what we think are the five best used sources for general trends and statistics on Facebook. To make it even sweeter for you, we have also shared our observations about the various sources, collated in a little table for easy reference. And if you are still undecided on where to start your intelligence gathering, we recommend that you start with the first source on our list, and then work your way down the list.

Table 2: Our List Of Five Best Used Sources for Facebook

1.	www.facebook.com	Hear it straight from the horses' mouth first: the official statistics released by Facebook. Timely and useful but basic information. Highly recommended as your first stop to help you sieve through the other data presented about Facebook by other sources.
2.	www.socialbakers.com	Good source of complimentary research analyses and infographics on Facebook trends. (Previously known as Facebakers). We like the classification by country/continent/city, brand and pages that aid easy searches. Data is updated frequently. We also like the fact there are signs that there are ongoing efforts to source for new and relevant data on Facebook.

3.	www.insidefacebook.com	Founded in 2006 some two years after Facebook was launched, there are good infographics available on the website for free, but you'll need to search for them. Alternatively, if you don't mind paying for data, there's plenty made available and these are not difficult to find. We like the fact that the authors and researchers are named – lends to data credibility.
4.	www.allfacebook.com	Data focus is limited to two important areas: traffic on Facebook Pages and apps (top/worst), with statistics searchable on a daily/weekly/monthly basis, but we find the limited data especially useful for marketers. Includes decent coverage of news and features dedicated to Facebook.
5.	www.mashable.com	Leading social networking news site. Lots of interesting insights and observations into the social networking community. More quality than quantitative data.

Gathering intelligence alone, however, does not make an effective recon exercise. What really matters is how we guerrillas make use of the intelligence gathered to figure out what's in it for our business: i.e., make meaningful conclusions from data. This is akin to having sufficient ammo for your weapons when launching an attack.

Now, this is where the going gets tough. The truth is, no one can tell you upfront what data is meaningful and what is not for your business. And it would be a fool's errand for us to try and make detailed conclusions for every business, since every business is different, with its own unique needs. And to be honest, no one will feel hard-pressed to make that final conclusion for you – not Facebook nor Google nor some other social media consultant or expert – well, at least not for free.

We may not be able to tell you what would or would not be meaningful for your business, but we can show you how we have made use of general data to get a sense of the magnitude of

Figure 1: Current active Facebook Users

Number of current active Facebook users: **955,000,000**		
March 2011: **664 million**	December 2011: **799 million**	March 2012: **835 million**
7.9 new registrations were made **every second** in 2010		
... close to **Half** of the **955 million users** log on to their Facebook account **every day**.		
543 million users access Facebook through **mobile devices**. And they are **twice as active** as non mobile Facebook users		

Source: Facebook Official Statistics; www.internetworldstats.com

Facebook's influence on brand awareness or information sharing, and to get tips on to carry out an effective Facebook marketing campaign. This is the objective of any recon exercise. To show you what we mean, let's start with some basics statistics, and work our way from there. Let's first work through these general trends in Figure 1 to draw some general conclusions:

1. Facebook is fastest growing social media tool — ever

Facebook is undeniably the world's leading social media tool – ever. It currently has a staggering following of some 950 million active users. That's 950,000,000 in numerals – no other social media comes close. To give you a sense of the scale, let's take a look at how this number compares with the total number of Internet users in the world. As of December 2010, there are more than 2 billion Internet users worldwide (source: International Telecommunication Union, ITU). This roughly works out to mean 37% of all Internet users are Facebook users. That's a pretty high following, and this trend is unprecedented in the history of website usage. In terms of website popularity, Facebook consistently ranks among the Top Ten Most Visited Websites on the Internet alongside other website giants such as Google, YouTube, Yahoo! and Wikipedia.

You could argue that the measure of Facebook's popularity in terms of the volume of users is, at best, cursory. What is more telling about these Facebook figures is that the number of Facebook users has been growing at an astounding pace. Here's a quick snapshot of Facebook's growth: by the end of the year in which it was launched (2004), Facebook had close to one million active users. Three years later in 2007, the number of active users rose to 50 million. (Even search engine Google took a longer time to hit 50 million users.) At the start of last year, 2010, there were

337 million registered users. In year 2010, there were 7.9 new Facebook registrations in every second, which meant that by the end of the year 2010, the number of users rose by 74% to 585 million. And its growth does not seem to be stopping anytime soon. In just three months of year 2012 (March to June 2012), the number of users surpassed the 900 million mark – that's a record of eight straight years of incredible, double-digit growth, measured in millions, no less.

But this is really just the tip of the iceberg. Here's more on what we can learn from these statistics:

2. Frequent opportunities to connect with customers

In Figure 1, we highlighted that half of the 955 million current active Facebook users (defined as a user who returns to log on to Facebook within a month), close to half of them log on to their Facebook account every day. So when we guerrillas get excited, it isn't just the fast-growing numbers that makes us guerrillas excited. What makes us guerrillas sit up, is that many Facebook users are active users – users log in every day: around 522 million users. What's more, there are some 543 million users who access Facebook through mobile devices such as their smart phones, and these users are twice as active as non mobile users. There is great potential for further growth by mobile users. When we first started writing this book a year ago, the number of such users around 200 million – that was about a year ago!

What this means is that your customers are on Facebook each and every day, connecting with friends, looking for information, sharing stories and photographs, and so on. This means that we guerrillas have many opportunities to connect and engage our customers with our brands, each and every day, at any given point in time – perhaps as often as once a day.

Seen from a marketing point of view, this also means that we guerrillas would want to have fresh and authentic input available as often as possible to engage our target audience – something that was not necessary in conventional static advertisements. Now, which other marketing tool provides you with this same opportunity?

Figure 2: User Age and Top Brands

72.5% of Facebook users are between the age of **13 and 34 years**
Coca Cola is the top brand in Facebook in 2011, with 4 new fans per second*

2. Disney
3. Starbucks
4. Oreo
5. Red Bull
6. Converse
7. Converse All Star
8. Skittles
9. Playstation
10. iTunes

*Source: www.thenextweb.com

3. Why engaging a young audience is useful

The majority of Facebook users are between the age of 13 and 34 (72.5%). Does age matter, and would this be considered good or bad news for a Guerrilla Facebook Marketer? It can go both ways. It's like giving a solider a hand grenade. Applied well, a hand grenade can carry out what it was meant to do. Handled wrongly, and it can backfire.

As we see it, there are two broad advantages of engaging a young audience:

1. We get a chance to grow our brand presence as our Facebook customers grow
2. We get a chance to keep our brands relevant to future generations

Since Facebook centers on relationship building, there's no time like the present to start the brand awareness building process, as well as to start building up a loyal fan base for our businesses. We like the idea of growing with our customers on Facebook – we see it as a way of infiltrating our target customers in a meaningful way in the long run.

We have deliberately presented information about the Top Ten Brands on Facebook vis-à-vis age profiles of Facebook users to help you make some connections between seemingly random pieces of information.

What we have observed is that a Facebook marketing strategy can help keep brands relevant to the next generation of consumers in the long run, when run well. Brands with more than a century of history are still making it a priority to remain relevant to the youth of today. Take a moment to consider this co-relation: despite the seemingly youngish population dominating Facebook, long-standing brands – notably Coca Cola (dates back to 1886), Oreo (1912), and Disney (1923) stand on par with "newer" brands such as Red Bull (1987), Starbucks (1971), Victoria's Secret (1977) and iTunes (2003) as Facebook's Top Ten

Brands in 2010. Could this be the result of coincidence, or the result of a deliberate strategy by these brands to secure relevance to future generations of consumers?

The third and final point we want to make about the age profiling of Facebook is pretty obvious, but is sometimes glossed over. Percentages don't really matter when it comes to Facebook users. Simply because there are so many Facebook users, it does not really matter even if your target age group makes up less than 1% of the 955 million users, or accounts for the majority 72.5%. You are still going to reach out to a sizable audience who is willing to connect and listen to you. Don't just take our word for it – do the math for yourself.

Figure 3: Top Ten Countries

Top Ten Countries on Facebook
(Oct 2010-March 2011)*

1. USA (152.2 million)
2. Indonesia (35.2 million)
3. UK (28.9 million)
4. Turkey (26.4 million)
5. Philippines (22.7 million)
6. India (22.1 million)
7. Mexico (21.9 million)
8. France (21 million)
9. Italy (18.4 million)
10. Canada (17.4 million)

*Source: www.socialbakers.com

4. Instant global reach

The dawn of Internet marketing has opened up instant global reach to many businesses, and Facebook is definitely one of them. Outside the US, both European and Asian countries feature equally in the top ten list, with one in every four users on Facebook based outside the US. This being said, we will readily admit that the attraction of instant global reach by Facebook no longer holds the same enticement as it did some 15 years ago. In fact, many marketers today assume that instant global reach as a given, considering the other web-based marketing options such as emails, blogs and websites. Still, we decided that it would be useful to highlight Facebook's global reach, and more importantly, to have this data on hand for your convenience.

If you are after data on a specific country, continent or city, we recommend you check out www.socialbakers.com – there are 213 countries listed on that website. This is by far the most extensive we have come across. The data is available on a weekly, monthly and six-monthly basis.

One general point we have observed about the profiling of users across countries is that the profiles can change from month to month. Users in the USA have consistently ranked #1 since Facebook was founded in 2004, with a significant portion of users residing in and around New York City. Not that nationality or country of origin matters all the time, since one can choose to connect locally with those who matter, or connect to hundreds on global scale, depending on business needs.

Figure 4: Friends and the "Like" Button

An average Facebook user has **130** friends
The "Like" Button is clicked on **6 times per day** per user

*source: www.facebook.com

No recon of Facebook would be complete without mention of Facebook's signature functions, namely the Friend function and the ubiquitous "Like" button. The fact that it is no secret that many know how the "Like" button is clicked on 6 times per day per user tells us something powerful – many different interest groups have their eyes on the little "Like" function.

5. The multiplier effect of "Like"

As marketers, we know and recognize the value of viva voce recommendations. Traditionally, word of mouth recommendations are made in person and are passed from one person to another. Its pace of passing on information is limited to the pace at which a person passes on the information to another, in other words, slowly. But technology - in particular the Internet and emails - has accelerated the rate in which word of mouth recommendations are passed on – information today can be virally passed on to hundreds and thousands with a simple click of a button within a short period of time.

Facebook users are not just logging on to Facebook to connect with friends. They are also logging in to find out what else is out there – according to their friends, that is. Research has shown that Facebook users between the ages of 13-34 are more likely to spend more time on social media like Facebook than on traditional media like TV, radio or newspapers for information, news, updates, reviews and discussions. They are also more likely to trust their friends' recommendations and reviews. Since this has a direct impact on brand awareness, it therefore becomes important for us to understand how information is passed on in Facebook.

Facebook has many marketing weapons we particularly like, of which the "Like" function (pun intended) gets our two thumbs up. In Facebook, when users come across something that they like, be it a service or product, they can choose to share it with their friends by a simple click of the "Like" option. When they do so, their preferences can in turn be seen by all their friends instantly on their newsfeed page, triggering off what we describe as the multiplier "Like" effect. Some Facebook experts describe this as information going "viral". This is the basis of a viral marketing campaign.

If numbers convince you more than our words, here's the math to get a sense of the speed and scale at which the "Like" effect spreads in Facebook. The average Facebook user has 130 friends. On average, one "Like" recommendation can be potentially viewed by another 130 friends within seconds of its posting, and in turn can be viewed by friends' friends, and so on. This multiplier effect of "Like" is one of the unique selling points about marketing on Facebook – no matter how you choose to interpret what users mean when they click on the "Like" button. Can you see why the "Like" function is one of our favorites?

Facebook itself also keeps a tight watch on the "Likes" of their users. The information gathered about "Likes" is undoubtedly sought after by developers, marketers and businesses the world over, and we discuss this further as one of the guerrilla Facebook marketing weapons in Chapter 4.

Word of mouth recommendations via Facebook keep getting better for guerrilla marketers. In addition to the "Like" option, friends can post their comments or start discussions on their profile pages in response to "Likes" – such conversation starters also serve to pass information quickly from user to user. For instance, the two most discussed products on Facebook in 2010 were the iPad and the iPhone 4 – some 25 million posts, comments, reviews and Likes were recorded for these two products. In the same year, Apple surpassed Microsoft in terms of market capitalization. This is a coincidence, or the result of a deliberate marketing strategy?

Even the strongest critics of Facebook cannot deny the unsurpassed supremacy Facebook has when it comes to passing on information. As guerrillas, we like it too – very much indeed.

Figure 5: Page Interactions and Apps Installation

There are over **900 million** pages, groups, events and community pages Facebook users interact with... an average Facebook user connects with **80** of them
20 million apps are installed each day, dominated by game developers and mobile applications*

*Source: www.allfacebook.com

6. Plenty of choice for users, plenty of work for marketers

With over 900 million pages, groups, events and community pages, there's plenty of choice for a user, considering that on average, a Facebook user connects with 80 of them (which is a lot). What this also means for us guerrillas is that we certainly have our work cut out for us.

So when we choose to build relationships with our customers on Facebook by holding meaningful and authentic conversations, this requires work over a period of time, since relationships seldom happen overnight. This also means we need to be prepared to channel sufficient resources to stay updated and relevant when we choose to launch a Facebook marketing campaign. Here's some food for thought if you are exploring the option of carrying out a Facebook marketing campaign: there usually is a direct correlation between poor Fan response and unmatched resources when carrying out a Facebook marketing campaign.

There is a plus side to the idea of having community pages and groups for like-minded interests. Facebook users sign up to connect with like-minded people on such pages. This means that when you engage your customers on Facebook, you are engaging with like-minded individuals who have chosen to connect with your brand. This gathering of like-minded people marks a significant shift in the way we carry out ad campaigns in the Facebook era. Gone are the days when the objective of marketing campaigns was to attract attention. These days, marketing campaigns need to be content driven – if the content is useful, thoughtful, sincere and consistent, there will naturally be a following. And the following will consist of people who like your brand. Your followers will provide you with instant feedback as they talk about their likes and respond to your advertisements and other marketing strategies. For example, in a 2010 survey conducted by social media consultant ExactTarget, 40% of their respondents indicated that they clicked on the "Like" button to receive discounts and promotions. That is a telling sign: if you offer something tangible for your target audience in return for their response, say a discount or a promotion, you are more likely to solicit a response and increase your chance of converting readers into consumers.

7. The power of apps

To date, the most popular applications (apps) on Facebook are dominated by game developers, mobile application providers (e.g. Facebook for iPhone, BlackBerry, android), and reviews (e.g. yelp, reviews). For more detailed information, we like the data provided by www.allfacebook.com that tracks 1,500 apps on a daily, weekly and monthly basis. If you just want a complete list of apps, www.insidefacebook.com claims to have the most updated list. There is a more detailed discussion on apps as a weapon in Chapter 4.

Why are we interested in apps? At a basic level, apps provide a way for marketers to gain information about its users. This is because users need to volunteer some data about themselves, in order to install an app on Facebook. The fact that there are 20 million apps installed each day is a sure indication of a user's willingness to volunteer data in exchange for a service. The popularity of apps also provides us with an indication of what users are using Facebook for. Need we add that the data gained from volunteered data is a minefield for marketers all around the world?

Introducing... Analytic Tools

As marketers, we are understandably fixated on finding out what our customers want. What do our customers want, and how do we get that information? Facebook has a unique culture that has a strong emphasis on data analysis, advertisement optimization and target audience. It is a culture we guerrillas strongly identify with. To this end, there are a couple of useful analytic tools one can use. These analytic tools help marketers gain better real-time insight that can help customer identification and profiling. These analytical tools will be discussed in detail in the later chapters of this book, but since we are on the topic of data analysis, we thought it best to first make mention of it here.

Facebook Recon:

1. Facebook is fastest growing social media tool—ever
2. Frequent opportunities to connect with customers
3. Why engaging a young audience is useful
4. Instant global reach
5. The multiplier effect of "Like"
6. Plenty of choice for users, plenty of work for marketers
7. The power of apps

CHAPTER 3

RULES OF ENGAGEMENT

When we first signed up for a Facebook account, the first thing that struck us was how clean and neat a Facebook profile looked like. There were no flashing banners or distracting advertisements that we have come to be accustomed to when visiting most websites and blogs. In Facebook, the placement of ads on a Page is limited to a column on the right hand side of a Page. This leaves us with plenty of white space to create the kind of Facebook experience we want.

By keeping the interface simple, Facebook sends a very clear message to its users and businesses alike: users have a choice. Users get to choose the content they want to see and read. Users get to choose the associations they want to make. Users get to choose the information they wish to publicly share. Users also get to decide, on their own terms, when and how they want to connect with their friends, other fans and businesses. Users are also at liberty to delete or unsubscribe to business Pages that they no longer want to be associated with. There are no distracting messages to cloud these choices – the user is free to choose what they want, when they want, and how they want it.

Permission marketing vs. interruption marketing

Guerrillas know that the key to understanding marketing is to understand how humans relate to marketing and how marketing relates to humans. Consumers nowadays fiercely guard their time and attention, yet never before have consumers felt this bombardment by interruption marketing. In interruption marketing, consumers are viewed as passive participants in the marketing process. Interruption marketing typically relies on attention-seeking or shock tactics to entice consumers to buy. But because today's consumers are constantly bombarded with marketing messages, interruption marketing has conversely lowered the chance of persuading the consumer to buy. Think of all the advertisements you have to sit through before you get to watch the ending of your favorite drama series. There is simply too much noise. It has become utterly impossible to remember all the messages, let alone act on them.

Permission marketing is a stark departure from interruption marketing, as described by Seth Godin, online promoter and author of 12 bestsellers. In permission marketing, businesses focus on building relationships with consumers over time, so as to win permission to market to the consumers. In the process of relationship building, consumers would willingly share information about themselves, their spending threshold, and so on. Permission marketing is a very powerful marketing tool, if only one knew how to harness it.

Facebook as a whole operates from the same premise as permission marketing. Facebook users get to decide what kind of

Facebook experience they want to have. They get to decide who and which businesses they want to connect with, and what kind of information they want to share with businesses. Facebook users are active participants. They are not just going to sit there and watch your big budget advertisement and make a purchase as the result of feeling impressed. They know they have a choice. They can walk away, and will walk away.

Permission marketing and Facebook marketing are relatively new concepts to marketers. To us guerrillas, they offer a fresh perspective on marketing that excites us. Like all things new, we start by defining some rules to help us along:

Rule #1: "Permission to make contact, Sir"

In Facebook, it starts and ends here.

When it comes to prospecting in Facebook, there is only one starting point: seeking consent to make contact. Guerrillas know this. They know that if they do not overcome this first hurdle, there is no alternative for them. The war – not just the battle - is over. In Facebook, they won't get access to customers if they do not have their permission to make contact. They won't be able to turn visitors into fans, and fans into customers.

The thing about guerrillas is that they are not handicapped just because there are barriers to entry. Instead, the barriers push guerrillas to try new ways of doing things. So in Facebook, guerrillas adopt new rules to engage their customers. They do this because they know that once permission to make contact with Facebook users is given, this will unlock the floodgates: some 522 million daily active users and counting.

Seeking and gaining consent is paramount in Facebook because it leads to access of information. Once consent is given, businesses can access pre-determined information (e.g. demographics, location, preferences, likes, friends' lists). Gaining consent is also one step closer to sales generation. In a fan's mind, the question after consent is not whether they should buy, but when, how, and in what quantities.

Rule #2: Page over Ads

Facebook and Guerrilla Marketing share many values in common. Let's take a quick step back to recall what Guerrilla Marketing is all about:

What is Guerrilla Marketing?

Guerrilla Marketing relies on time, energy, imagination and creativity rather than budget and/or other conventional marketing methods to make a valuable impression about a business.

The Guerrilla brand originated from a passionate belief that those with limited resources can still compete—and win—in a level playing field with other companies—as long as they are armed with the right weapons and knowledge.

In Guerrilla Facebook Marketing, it is really not how much money that you invest in Facebook that determines the outcome of your marketing campaign. What matters is how much time, energy and attention you invest on your Facebook Page to build relationships with your fans. These are your prime investments. The more you spend in these areas, the higher your chances of building up strong relationships with your fans will be.

If you wish to approach Facebook simply as a medium to blast your ads, you can do so – Facebook offers businesses the possibility of posting ads to their Facebook users. More on Facebook ads as a Guerrilla weapon is covered in Chapter 4 of this book.

But this is not the way of the Guerrilla Facebook Marketer. This is also not what Facebook was designed to do.

Customers today want to buy from businesses that have earned their confidence, that display respect for them, that are recommended by trusted sources such as friends, and share their values. When customers find businesses that offer them these things, they won't mind paying more for it. It is no longer just about price.

Hence, advertising does not give you precedence in Facebook. The starting point of engagement in Facebook is therefore not an ad, but your Page. Hence our rule, Page over Ads. If you are new to Facebook, you may wish to skim ahead to Chapter 4 on weapons to learn more about Facebook Pages first. On Facebook, having a big advertising budget isn't necessarily going to convert visitors into fans, and fans into customers. Conversely, not many features on Facebook come with a price tag. In Chapter 4 of this book, there are some 25 Guerrilla weapons in Facebook featured, out of which at least 20 weapons are free to use without the need to pay for anything other than your time, energy and attention.

Rule #3: Identify what motivates fans to connect

In the past, marketing communication was a one-way street. Businesses used to hold monologues with their customers: they spoke, and their customers listened.

Facebook's dynamic platform, however, has transformed the way businesses communicate with their customers. Today, fans and customers are engaged in two-way dialogues. Businesses can post updates, hold events and conduct polls. Fans and visitors have the option of co-creating content on Pages by uploading images and videos, leaving comments or engaging in discussion groups. They are also co-creating content for businesses when they participate in marketing events such as contests or polls, share reviews, external links or engage in discussion groups with other fans. In other words, they are connecting.

Making connections is central to any relationship. Associations, linkages and sharings lead to forming bonds or unions. This is what making connections are about. Facebook offers users many opportunities to make connections – with friends, other fans, and with businesses. And since it is important feature in Facebook, it is useful for guerrillas to first understand what motivates people to connect with others on Facebook.

Some people are motivated to connect with others because they are looking for social contact. For example, looking to find companionship, love or friendship, or to catch up with family and old friends. Some people are motivated to connect for acceptance. For example, joining and participating in interest groups to feel included or sense of belonging. Other people could be motivated to connect for status. For example, sharing one's life achievements or success to feel important. Or to connect based on a shared cause or idealism. For example, sharing opinions, reviews, comments and external links to influence friends to band together for a social cause. Then there are those who connect for sheer entertainment. For example, posting funny videos, images or jokes for a good laugh. And there are those who make connections for personal gain or benefit. For example, participating in events such as contests or giveaways for personal benefit, or for networking purposes.

Figure 6: Motivations to Connect in Facebook

Social Contact	Acceptance	Status
Looking to find love, companionship or friendship, or to catch up	Participating to feel included or for sense of belonging	Sharing life's achievements / successes
Idealism	**Entertainment**	**Personal Gain**
Banding together for social cause or justice	Posting funny videos, images or jokes	Participating for personal benefit

Now that you have some insight on what motivates people to connect with others on Facebook, how does this shape the way you would approach your Facebook strategy to make it more meaningful and authentic for your fans?

Rule #4: Follow the linear process of engagement

To transform prospects into engaged fans and finally to consensual customers, there is linear process to follow. We say "linear" because it is easier to go through the natural linear order. By allowing each stage run its course before proceeding to the next stage makes the process run much smoother.

Since we already know from Chapter 1 that the core of Facebook lies in relationships, we are going to approach Guerrilla Facebook Marketing in a similar way as we would approach starting a new relationship.

So let's just assume that you know what kind of person you would like to date and skip ahead to the part when you have found someone who interests you.

What do you do?

Well, you would put yourself out there. You let the other person know that you are available, and how to contact you – easily. In the book on Guerrilla Social Media Marketing, author Shane Gibson refers to this stage as the Discovery stage.

Stage 1: Discovery

Discovery refers to how easily people can find you - on Facebook and elsewhere. Do you have your contact details readily available? Is your Facebook business Page mentioned elsewhere – both online and offline? For example, on name cards, printed brochures and so on? Can you hold an event to generate buzz about your Facebook presence? If you already have an Internet presence, have you made the links between your external websites and Facebook? If you already have a following on your blog or twitter account, what can you do to entice your followers to follow you on Facebook? What is your Facebook presence like? Do you have a well set-up Page? Have you tried searching for your Page on google and on Facebook search itself? Can you get involved in Group Discussions? How can you get your current fans to recommend your Page to others? Will a viral marketing campaign work for you?

Stage 2: Introduction

The next step would be to let the other party know who you are. Note that at this stage, the other party may not be open or receptive to you, so the onus is on you to volunteer information about yourself. Let's call this stage the Introduction stage.

Introduction refers to your first impressions – in this case, it could be elsewhere – both offline as well as online – and not necessarily on Facebook. This is when you could share information about your background, where you are coming from, your preferences, and your likes. At this stage, it could feel like a monologue, but keep at it. Your aim is to establish trust and confidence in you and your brand. If you have played your cards right, the other party might be sufficiently interested to check you out, with or without you knowing. The key point is to keep your introduction non-committal by offering the other party options to choose from. Remember, the other party did not sign up for this. If you have an existing website or blog or YouTube video, why not start with those first? You would ensure that there is an option to follow you on Facebook from these links. Naturally, we have assumed that your Facebook and other online presence have been spruced up and ready for these all-important first impressions.

The objective of this Introduction stage is to take the first step in getting some consent from the other party, for instance, finding a way to contact the other party. This applies to any first meeting when the interested party would want to secure a way to continue connecting beyond the first introduction or meeting. Be open to many forms of contact - be it a business card, an email address, a twitter account name, a blog address, a telephone number, or - lucky you - you might even land yourself an address. By all means, use guerrilla weapons, such as a Sign-up feature, if you have to.

Nowhere – we repeat – nowhere in the introductions should there a sales pitch hidden somewhere. You do that now, and the game's over. You'll go home empty handed.

Stage 3: Interaction
Once you have that contact, the flirting dance can commence. This is the stage in which both parties get to know each other. No big surprises here, so we are just going to call this stage the Interaction stage.

Interaction marks the beginning of conversations. It is an exciting stage as the other party is warming up to you – and you know this because there has been some positive response on their end. After all, you have their attention now. In terms of strategy, think customized and personalized. For instance, invitations to events and to join discussions / interest groups that you moderate. Take note of their birthdays and make an event out of it. Offer the other party the option of coming to you. You could entice them by offering incentives to interact with you – free seminars, invitation-only previews, samplers, and the like. Have different landing tabs for visitors as opposed to fans: this helps them feel special, but not overwhelmed. Ask questions when you can. Seek clarifications, and confirm needs. If you can't ask questions, observe - this is how you can get the most out of your analytical tools. For instance, you could pay closer attention to the traffic generated on Facebook and elsewhere to identify links between traffic flows and their directions. Like in dancing, two parties are learning how each other's tempos go – so pay attention to how the other party is reacting to your advances by monitoring your Page traffic statistics.

Stage 4: Consent

If you have faithfully followed these stages, by now, the other party would be receptive to what you have to say. You are now in the position of power to influence the other party. Now is the time you would want to pull out your bigger guns: you might want to demonstrate value, offer solutions, or highlight benefits. You are drawing the other party in: you are going in for the kill.

The final stage in starting a new relationship is **consent**. Once consent is given, the most valuable act you as a business can do is to honor that consent of the other party. You can do this by providing regular authentic conversations, connecting with them on a regular basis, and giving genuine offers from time to time. Think loyalty programmes, exclusive fan offers, fans-only events. There's more on deepening relationships covered in Rules #5 and 6.

Discovery leads on to introductions, and then on to interactions, and finally, consent. If you follow this natural linear process and let each stage run its course, it makes the process of relationship building much easier.

Rule #5: The sale is no longer the end point

After the initial consent is sought and given, there's more.

You are now in a consensual, connected relationship. You are connected to the other party, and the other party is connected to you. You decide to take things further by getting hitched. Would you consider marriage the end point of your relationship? Absolutely not. In fact, getting hitched merely marks the beginning of a new and deeper relationship with the other party.

The same goes for your relationships with your consensual fans. With consent from your fans-turned customers, this marks the beginning of a new and deeper relationship between you and your fans. This is why we have Rule #5: the sale is no longer the end point.

So what do you do after a sales relationship is consensual? For a start, you follow-up after a sale. It could be as simple as checking to see if the goods had arrived on time, or whether the service was satisfactory. Guerrillas would take it a notch higher. They know people no longer surf the web just for information. They are logging on to social websites like Facebook to be heard. Guerrillas meet this need head on by asking for reviews – if fans had liked it, how about sharing their experience on the brand's Page? What about referrals? If they enjoyed the service, how about recommending it to their friends? What about connecting with other fans on your Page? If they like your brand, how about joining the Discussion Boards or fan clubs to meet and mingle with like-minded fans?

Rule #6: Fans cannot and should not be treated equally

Guerrillas recognise the value in repeat business from loyal customers – these are the ones who have accepted and enjoyed your brand, and are seeking to connect with your brand further. They are the ones who like your business culture. In other words, they too are looking to deepen their relationship with you, just as you are interested to deepen your relationship with them. Can it get any better than this?

The important rule when it comes to handling loyal fans is summed up in our sixth rule: fans cannot and should not be treated equally. A guerrilla marketer recognizes the importance of treating these loyal followers in special and unique ways so that they always feel especially loved and connected to you. Recall that in Rule #3, one of the motivations for users to connect with others is acceptance and social contact.

What are some special and exclusive ways to connect with your top fans? What will make them come back and revisit your Page day after day, participate in your discussions, and engage with you again and again? Why would they feel compelled to recommend or introduce your Page to their friends?

You could start with organizing exclusive promotions and discounts for select groups of fans at different times. But don't stop there. What about appointing your top fans to be spokespeople for the brand? Or inviting these top fans to be part of your testing bed for new products or services?

Finally, in some very successful brand relationships, some top fans can be eventually recruited to become part of a business, either working in the capacity of an employee or on projects in collaboration with a business.

These top fans are not only loyal consumers of your brand, but also willing to work with you to further your brand to others.

They are the best kind of customers you can have for your business.

---

6 Rules of Engagement

Rule #1: Permission to make contact, sir

Rule #2: Page over ads

Rule #3: Identify what motivates fans to connect

Rule #4: Follow the linear process of engagement

Rule #5: The sale is no longer the end point

Rule #6: Fans cannot and should not be treated equally

CHAPTER 4

FROM ADS TO APPS: 25 FACEBOOK-SPECIFIC GUERRILLA MARKETING WEAPONS

Guerrillas have a lot to give and share. To add on to the 200+ Guerrilla Marketing weapons identified for use in any Guerrilla Marketing campaign, we are offering guerrillas some 25 Facebook-specific weapons to choose from in this Chapter.

Some weapons can help you generate or manage your content on Facebook; other weapons can help you engage your fans to increase customer loyalty or help you build your fan base. Some weapons help you improve your brand awareness and online reputation; while other weapons help you publicize or spread the word around by way of word of mouth marketing.

So the first step towards choosing our weapons is to get to our observation post so that we can get to know what is out there in

Facebook in terms of features, tools and resources. Facebook is only as good as what we know about it. But even then, it's not over. It's not enough to just know what Facebook is about. We need to understand how Facebook works so that we can apply strategies in Facebook to forward our cause. We need to know what features we can use to forward our position. We need to know what tools are available so that we can use them to secure our position. And we need to know what resources are available that could help us defend our position, and which ones could compromise our position and backfire on us.

To do this, we will discuss each of the 25 weapons in detail, highlighting its functions and its applicability to us Guerrilla Marketers.

So let's begin. Weapon #1: Facebook Page

Weapon #1: Facebook Page

This is where it begins in Facebook – your Facebook Page. Your Facebook Page is best understood as the "official" representation of your business on Facebook. We say "official" because there are other ways to represent your business on Facebook, but most businesses would invariably opt to start with a Facebook Page first.

So what is a Facebook Page all about? A Facebook Page acts as an information broadcast system. It is public information that can be disseminated to anyone: information posted on your Facebook Page can be seen by anyone who has a Facebook account.

Page vs Profile?

At first glance, a Facebook Page is very similar to that of a personal Facebook Profile, but there are some crucial differences to take note of. Facebook Pages were designed for optimal use by businesses and organizations, while Facebook Profiles were designed to represent individuals. One of the criteria of starting a Facebook Profile is that it must be held under an individual's name. Organizations and businesses with Facebook Pages can have a number of administrators who can access and post updates on Facebook Pages. Administrators, however, need to have personal Facebook accounts in order to post updates on your business' Facebook Page. This has the effect of keeping Facebook Pages real – that is, that they are administered by real people. Facebook Profiles typically have only one administrator – the individual and the administrator is one and the same.

Another point to note about Facebook Profiles is that they have an upper limit of 5,000 friends, while there are no upper limits to the number of fans a Facebook Page can have. Lady Gaga, for instance, was the first living person in Facebook history to have more than 10 million fans on her Facebook Page. As your business will grow over time, this can be an important consideration when deciding between the two.

On your Facebook Page, you can leverage on the customized tabs function (Weapon #9) to determine what kind of content you wish to generate. For instance, you could post static information about your business such as contact details or links to your existing business website, or you could also choose to share photos or videos about your recent publicity campaign, feature reviews about your new products or services, or generate discussions about your business or brand. You could also administer polls or post questions to engage your fans – the opportunities are limitless.

> **Profile or Page?**
>
> Facebook Profiles: personal, used by individuals.
>
> Facebook Pages: used by authorized individuals of businesses & organizations; managed by administrators with personal Facebook profiles.

One point to note about your activity on your Facebook Page is that updates are automatically featured on your Wall. More of this is covered in Weapon #2. This has the intended effect of informing your fans what you have been up to on your Facebook Page.

Ten-Hut! Weapon Tip #1:

First things first: if you are a Facebook Freshie, spend some time first deciding on what kind of Facebook presence you want – do you want to create a Facebook Profile, a Facebook Group (Weapon #4), or a Facebook Fan Page (Weapon #5)?

Weapon #2: The Wall

The most dynamic element of your Facebook presence is your Wall. This is where a Facebook Page differs from traditional websites and other social media such as Twitter, YouTube or blogs. The Wall featured in Facebook summarizes your Facebook activity in one easy glance. Your Facebook Wall is highly interactive – this is where you build your community by posting questions, sharing photos and videos, gathering feedback, organizing events, and so on. You can adjust your privacy settings to permit your Facebook friends/ fans to function as an open forum – fans can post comments on your updates – or choose not to – depending on what you are trying to achieve.

Information dissemination & publicity tool

Your Wall is an extremely effective information dissemination and/ or publicity tool - any recent activity on your Facebook Page can be immediately viewed by your fans on their News Feed (see Weapon #3). For what's it is worth, you don't always need big demonstrations to engage your fans who visit your Wall: simple, small actions such as status updates, sharing photos or videos, or posting questions can be just as effective as a full-on product launch event. Think of it this way: if you are wooing someone, it's not always about wine, roses and expensive candlelight dinners. Small details, such as remembering how the person likes his or her morning coffee, or playing his or her favourite tune is just as important - if not more so, as we guerrillas like to believe so.

If you are a Facebook Freshie, we recommend that you read the following weapons (Weapons #3-8) in the corresponding order they are presented in this Chapter. For each weapon, we aim to discuss various basic functions that help us Guerrilla Marketers make our marketing campaigns more effective. If you are familiar with Facebook functions, you may wish to advance to Weapon #9 on Customized Tabs instead.

Weapon #3: News Feeds

The successful spread of information on Facebook lies within the News Feed function. The News Feed is a collection of short messages that streams recent activity on what is happening to your business on your friends/fan's News Feed Page. The News Feed appears on the first page of all Facebook users the moment they log in to their Facebook accounts. In web-speak, this is often referred to as the "landing page". This is where your friends/fans can get the latest updates on your business, and is certainly an effective way of publicizing events or new product launches.

News Feeds open a range of marketing ideas for guerrillas to launch. We guerrillas can make use of News Feeds to build relationships with our fans by streaming interest stories, making announcements about exclusive discounts or offers, holding marketing events, and so on. The key point is to keep your content ongoing: when we say that Facebook marketing happens best in small, incremental doses. It is here in your News Feed that sums it best for your Facebook marketing strategies.

How little updating is too little? How much is too much?

In Chapter 2, we highlighted that of the 955 million users, nearly half of them log onto Facebook every day. So if your idea of a Facebook marketing campaign is to engage your fans once every 6 months, your Facebook presence will take a long, long time to grow. If, however, you are updating your fans once every hour on the hour, we would be curious to know where you would be getting the tonnes of compelling content you would need in order to be updating once every hour on the hour. Perhaps you have launched an intense 48-hour marketing campaign. If you have what it takes -- we say why not – go for it.

While there are no hard and fast rules, we guerrillas would go out on a limb to suggest that an update once a day, or once a week sounds like a good middle-of-the-ground to take, but take into account your business' unique selling point. For example, if you are in the business of selling seasonal products such as Christmas trees, it might not make sense of you to be posting daily updates in the middle of summer… unless of course, you are selling Christmas Trees to Australians down under.

If you really want to drill down your attack to greater precision, you could strategically post your updates at times when you know your fans are most likely to log on. There are other weapons you could use as leverage, for example, Weapon #21: Analytics to discover the patterns of your visitors and fans to your Page. This way, you could increase your chances of getting your status updates featured on your fans' News Feeds.

You don't get to control the News Feed function of your fans

While the News Feed function is important way of reaching out to your fans, you need to bear in mind that you don't get to control what appears on your fans' News Feeds. Understanding how the News Feed function works is important as it would impact the way you approach your marketing plan on Facebook.

For instance, your status updates could just be one of the many status updates fed into your fans' News Feeds. In addition, not all status updates feed directly into everybody's News Feeds. Hence, we would also caution against assuming that the News Feed function on Facebook alone would get you the undivided attention you are hoping for from your fans.

There is a lot of noise in Facebook, and it takes more than that to get someone's attention on Facebook.

Not "new" information

One other thing to note about News Feeds is that the information reflected in the News Feed is not "new" in itself – it is simply a collection of information that has been voluntarily given by users – be it an update on your status, uploading of photos, videos, or comments left on someone else's Wall. So while News Feeds can help reiterate or generate greater awareness about a certain event or brand, it does not, and would not, provide new or additional information. Not that this is a huge problem to us guerrillas, but there is a subtle difference that you need to be aware of.

Weapon #4: Facebook Groups

Facebook Groups are small community groups banded together with a common denomination, such as school, geographical location, city, workplace or region on the basis of common interest or affiliation. Individuals can be added to groups through recommendations by friends. Compared with Facebook Pages, membership to Facebook Groups is exclusive; in that its entry to membership is limited by invitation only – this means that the general public may not know of the Group unless s/he has been invited or recommended by someone within the circle to join the Group.

> Facebook Groups provide the natural setup for identifying and understanding the needs of your niche market

Encouraging group discourse

The main elements of Facebook Groups are designed to encourage group discourse. Facebook Group members can engage in group chats - up to a maximum of 250 members, be on the same private mass messaging list for event invitations - messages that get sent into a user's inbox- share videos, photos and comments among Group members. The new feature of Facebook Groups that is not available on personal Facebook Profiles or Pages is the ability to share documents with other members of the same group. This new feature opens up new ways for marketers and group members to share and brainstorm ideas.

From a Guerrilla Marketer's perspective, Facebook Groups are the closest setup to focus group discussions. The setup provides businesses with a focused way of seeking and receiving constructive feedback on a personal level – *sans* the logistics involved when arranging for face-to-face focus group discussions. Although it does not mean that the effort involved is any less. You still need to have a plan of engagement knocked out. You still need to allocate an administrator or moderator to oversee the discussions on a regular basis.

Facebook Groups provide the natural setup for identifying and understanding the needs of your niche market – you have a group of interested fans, and they are sharing their preferences, what works for them and what does not. As for you… you exhibit your sincerity in listening carefully to what your fans have to say. You ask questions. You seek feedback. You seriously consider adopting sound suggestions or proposals that your fans have made. Your fans feel heard and understood. Essentially, you are doing what Facebook was set up to do: you are making connections with your fans, and they too are connecting with you.

Group vs. Page

What is the difference between Facebook Groups and Facebook Pages? The recon has been done for you:

1. Visibility. Facebook Pages are visible to all Facebook users. Anyone can join or sign up to be a Fan of a Page. Membership to Groups is selective – users have to be invited to join Groups. Only content on Pages come up in web engine searches; content in Groups are not searchable in the public domain.

2. Surveillance. Activity on Facebook Fan Pages can be monitored quantitatively by Facebook's analytics, Facebook Insights or some other analytics tool, while activity on Facebook Groups cannot be monitored in quantitative ways. Facebook Insights is explored in detail as Weapon #21: Facebook Analytics.

3. <u>Term and Scale.</u> Pages are better suited for businesses that are looking to build long-term relationships with larger groups of people. Facebook Groups permit membership restriction and are therefore better suited for smaller-scale groups of people who are gathered together to discuss a shorter-term project, for example, a specific or time-sensitive topic.

4. <u>Level of commitment.</u> As the word suggests - members of a Group "join" a Group – in other words, they "join" to participate more actively, for example, participate in discussions and events, as compared to fans who simply need to Like a Page to become connected to it. In terms of expected commitment, fans of Pages are more likely to participate less on Pages compared to participating in Groups, but this point can be moot. Tread with some caution.

5. <u>App aptitude.</u> Pages can support a wide range of apps: from customized page tabs (See Weapon #8: Customized Page Tabs) to quirky, customized apps such as order apps - we recommend taking a look at Pizza Hut's Facebook order app. Facebook Groups, however, can share events and send invites to their members' inboxes, as long as the group membership remains under 5,000 members.

There are pros and cons to creating Pages as opposed to Groups. Both have their strengths and weaknesses.

Our question to you is, what is stopping you from creating both?

Some businesses do launch both, depending on the kind of marketing campaign they wish to launch, the level of participation they are targeting for from their fans, and their available resources. For instance, if you sell specialized fishing equipment, you may launch a Page promoting the activity and your business, while maintaining a Group to discuss the finer points of fishing among enthusiasts.

Weapon #5: Facebook Fan Pages

Fan Pages are set up by fans who are not authorized to create Pages. A Fan Page is not the same as a Page. Setting up Facebook Fan Pages is the only alternative available for fans to post their own information about a business, celebrity or personality without impersonating the real business or person. In social media lingo, this type of content is typically classified as user-generated content or UGC, as it is sometimes referred to.

Fan Pages deserve your attention

Why have we identified Fan Pages as a separate weapon? It is because we guerrillas recognise the value of giving power to the masses. Fan Pages can be a powerful tool in Facebook. Fan pages in Facebook have been notoriously known to gather fans and like-minded users into action – be it to boycott something, or to raise funds, or to bring about a change. We guerrillas simply cannot dismiss something this powerful. If Fan Pages can influence behaviour, we want to explore how we can be part of it.

If there is a Fan Page created about your business in Facebook, we feel it deserves your attention. Fan Pages can be a hot bed of marketing research for a business. This is where fans share their comments, ideas and preferences. It is not uncommon to find fans creating images or even sharing videos made by themselves about the topic. Such user-generated content is amazing. Where else are you going to get organic, raw and unadulterated feedback about your business?

In addition, you can choose to participate or be involved in the Fan Page as well. This is what some celebrities or well-known personalities have done, some to good success in terms of building up their reputation and branding. As for you, the business owner, when you interact with your fans, you are not only engaging with your prospective or current customers, you are also creating links back to your official business page, therefore increasing your Facebook presence.

Weapon #6: Facebook Apps

Apps are the heart of Facebook. You can't talk about an effective Facebook Page or Group without the mention of apps. Facebook applications – apps – are tools created by Facebook developers as well as third party developers to offer users the ability to customize their Facebook experience the way they like it, without the need to have training in using software or specialized programming skills.

There are apps for everything – and we mean everything – you can think of. If you think apps are just social games, think again! To us Guerrilla Marketers, the Facebook apps we love are those that help us in our marketing efforts:

Facebook apps we guerrillas love:

- Analytical Tools (e.g. Facebook Insights—Weapon #21): apps that collate rich and up-to-date behavioural and demographic data
- Automatic Content Generators (e.g. Feed Burners— Weapon #15): apps that help you generate automatic content for News Feeds
- Promotions Organizers (e.g. Weapon #17): apps that create and administer publicity events such as sweepstakes or contests for fans

These easily available apps provide decent ammunition for any Guerrilla Marketing campaign. Many apps are free, while some come at a price.

If you have deeper pockets and are willing to expend more resources to enhance your Facebook presence, you can consider developing a customized app for your business. You can choose to outsource this to a third-party developer, or engage in a little DIY - you will need to learn Facebook's Markup Language to do this. If you decide to engage in some DIY, there are a number of online tutorials you can follow to help you learn how to come up with your own app.

App woes

One issue about selecting apps is that there is no comprehensive listing of apps for you to browse through and choose from. This is simply because there are hundreds of thousands of apps to choose from.

Another problem with apps is, how do you find apps that work best for you? In part due to the rapid number of apps that can be developed on any given day, identifying or searching for appropriate apps that work for you will be tricky, especially if you are a Facebook Freshie. Here are our tips on how to get your app radar going:

1. Start by browsing Facebook's apps list at www.facebook.com/apps/directory.php. This list is non-exhaustive but it is a good start.
2. Check out what apps your friends / fans are using as indicated on the postings on their walls. This does means that your app radar would be limited to what apps your friends or fans are using.

3. Ask around: rely on recommendations or by word of mouth.
4. Use the general search function in Facebook to look for apps by keywords.
5. Read up Facebook's official Developers page at http://developers.facebook.com/docs/guides/canvas/
6. Use our hints: we have taken the liberty of identifying and sharing with you our favourite apps in this book!

Ten-Hut! Weapon Tip #2:

Apps, plug-ins and add-ons or extensions basically carry out the same function, but the scope of ability varies. For a discussion on the differences and how it can impact your Facebook Page and online presence, turn to Weapon #16 on Plug-ins.

Weapon #7: Call-To-Action Buttons

As Guerrilla Marketers, we are especially delighted with the range of Call-to-Action buttons available on Facebook. This is all part of the connection element that Facebook provides so well for use between users and content providers.

Call-to-Action buttons are like adding additional firepower to your guerrilla weapons without increasing your overall budget. They can be easily included in your external websites or on to your Facebook Pages to boost your Facebook presence.

On Facebook, Call-To-Action buttons have two effects: (1) they improve the visibility of your brand or business by way of word of mouth from your fans and (2) they help encourage relationship building between you and a visitor by making it real easy for the visitor to your Facebook Page or website to convert into a fan or follower.

There are plenty of Call-to-Action buttons on Facebook. Here are our favorites:

- The Like Button
- The Become a Fan Button
- The Follow Us on Facebook Button
- The Comment Function
- The Share Function
- The Recommend Button

The Like Button

We guerrillas really like the Like Button. In Chapter 2 on Facebook Recon, we have already sung praises of the Like Button, and here we are again, in awe of this simple but effective button. Facebook's Like button appeals to a guerrilla's reliance on energy, imagination and creativity rather than budget. The Like button provides positive feedback on your Facebook Page: it is direct marketing response at its simplistic best. When your fans click on the Like button, your Page's visibility is boosted among your fans' friends, and friends of friends, and so on. On average, more than 2 billion posts are liked and commented on in a day. Instant exposure, minimum fuss.

The Become a Fan & Follow Us on Facebook Buttons

The Become a Fan button is another hot favourite. If your Page has got the goods, get your visitors to convert into fans. The "Follow Us on Facebook" button works in a similar way – it enables you to feature this Call-to-Action on your existing websites, for example, blogs or corporate websites, generating more interest to both your Facebook Page as well as to your external website.

Once a Facebook user clicks on the Like button or Become a Fan button of your Page, that user begins a relationship with that Page – although s/he need not be a friend to receive status updates from your business, s/he is now connected to your business' Page, and along with it, he will receive News Feed updates from that business page.

The best part about the Like button is that there are no limits on how many Likes a user can have! On average, the Like button is clicked on six times per day per user. That's 6 x 955,000,000 times per day.

The Like button has also been recognized as an effective tool in lead generation for marketers. For example, you can get visitors to your Page to sign up by Liking your Page. Other commonly-used phrases include "Like Us to Find out More", or "Like This Page Before the Deal is Gone".

The Comment or Share Buttons

More than that, other Call-to-Action buttons, such as Comment or Share, encourage your fans to interact with your Facebook Pages, therefore providing opportunities for you to deepen your relationships with your fans – getting to know them better, identifying their needs and their preferences.

If you do choose to include the Comment button on your Page, do note that comments can positively or negatively affect your brand's reputation. We discuss this in Weapon #9 on Discussion Boards.

The Recommend Button

Another similar function to the Like button is the Recommend function. Fans and visitors to your Page can recommend your Page to their friends. A variation to this function is the referral – encouraging your fans to recommend your Pages to their friends. The Share function is similar, permitting your fans to share what they have found interesting or exciting about your business to their friends. This word of mouth marketing technique to gain greater web presence is a sure-winner to us guerrillas.

Call-to-Action functions are not limited to buttons. Facebook takes this idea much farther as it also has a number of other functions we Guerrillas can use to engage our fans in different ways. More on this in Weapons #9-13.

Weapon #8: Customized Tabs

Customized tabs play an important role when creating your unique business Page in Facebook. As our heading suggests, the tabs on your Facebook Pages can be customized to meet your specific needs. If you are not familiar with Facebook tabs, think of tabs like having separate pages on your website. Depending on what you need, you can choose to highlight or feature certain content on Facebook using this feature. For instance, a company might choose to feature fun or informal ways of engaging its customers through certain tabs in Facebook, for instance, a poll or photo tab, while maintaining a more "serious" or formal corporate image on one of the tabs, for instance, a Info tab.

To make it sweeter for you, we have identified a number of customizable tabs (Weapons #9-13) that we think are especially useful for guerrillas, namely Discussion Boards (Weapon #9), Reviews (Weapon #10), Event Sharing and Invitation (Weapon

#11), Question and Polls (Weapon #12) and Photo and Video Sharing (Weapon #13).

Ten-Hut! Weapon Tip #3:

In Facebook, tabs are treated like separate pages. If you want to monitor which tabs are most viewed by fans and visitors to your Page, then you would want to create separate tabs for various functions. Facebook Insights track tabs separately to offer you interesting insights into which tabs are most popular among your fans.

Static FBML

To customize tabs, you will need to use the Static FBML (Facebook Mark-Up Language) app. The Static FBML app is by far one of the most used apps in Facebook – there are more than 106 million monthly users at the time of writing. In sum, this is the tool you need to use if you want to customize the look and design of the tabs on your Facebook Page. You can also decide which landing tab your fans or visitors will land first when they first access your Facebook Page. To customize tabs, you will need to have some knowledge of how to edit standard HTML codes. There are many online tutorials and guides available on the Internet. The Static FBML tool also permits you to format and embed videos and many other features on to your Facebook Page.

Ten-Hut! Weapon Tip #4:

If you are like most entrepreneurs with little or no knowledge of HTML codes, you can still try to create your own tabs. The truth is, you are not alone. Many Facebook Pages were developed through trial and error. While Facebook does not provide much assistance by way of guides or tutorials, you will find plenty of free advice, guides and online tutorials available on the net.

Weapon #9: The Discussion Board Tab

Discussion Boards are like focussed two-way conversations on Facebook. These Boards can let you know what your fans are thinking about, and what they like. In return, you can seek instantaneous feedback on your products or services without having to conduct lengthy focus group discussions. In other words, Discussion Boards deepen the involvement between you and your fans. Discussion Boards are common for Facebook Groups, but it does not mean that a Facebook Page cannot have a meaningful Discussion Board.

Discussion Boards vs. Groups

For example, popular third party Facebook game app developer, Zynga, has a number of Facebook Fan Pages with active Discussion Boards. These Discussion Boards bring together gamers who are interested to share and compare notes about their progress in the Zynga games they play, in a meaningful manner. At the same time, there are also a number of Facebook Groups in which like-minded Zynga gamers can gather together to share notes and help one another for specific outcomes.

Cutting both ways

Something to think about Discussion Boards: as with any form of free response, Discussion Boards can cut both ways. Some fans unhappy with your product or service may choose to voice out their unhappiness openly and publicly on your Discussion Boards.

> As with any form of free response, Discussion Boards can cut both ways – some fans unhappy with your product or service may choose to voice out their unhappiness openly and publicly on your Discussion Boards.

You could choose to manage feedback in two ways: (1) leave the comments as it is, and let other fans decide for themselves, or (2) delete them and cause more irritation to unhappy fans who then feel as though their opinions, in this case, discontent, is being ignored. The same goes for other open-ended free response functions such as Comment.

What you could do is to indicate openly on your Page your policy regarding moderation of comments on your Discussion Board. For instance, you could specify that there could be filters for spam, hate threats or harassing behaviour. Such behaviour will not be tolerated. After all, you can't always depend on your fans to behave rationally at all times, but you can certainly tell your fans what kind of content would be removed. This way, when rules are flouted, you are simply carrying out what you said you would do. If they do not agree, well, then they are free to leave. This is far better than the damage control you would have to do when fans realise that their comments have been unfairly deleted.

Managing Discussion Boards

Another consideration before including a Discussion Board on your Page is to figure out how much resources you have to maintain this particular line of attack.

In particular, think through how much time you think you would want to spend on moderating or managing your Discussion Board. The best way to determine this is to think about your policy regarding the timeliness of your responses to fan posts. What is considered a reasonable response rate? Every hour? Every day? Once every two days?

Also think about how much resources you have to manage your Discussion Board. Will you be running this as a one-person show? If so, in this world of global connectedness, who will mind your Discussion Board at 4am in the morning? Who will handle the Discussion Board when a crisis strikes? Do you have the resources to consider enlisting someone as the moderator of your Discussion Board?

If this function does not appeal to you, remember that you are the General of your battalion. Discussion Boards and Comments are options you can choose to omit from your Facebook Page. Do recall that we have mentioned that tabs can be customized: if it isn't there, it won't be missed.

Weapon #10: The Review Tab

A Review tab is another option you can choose to include on your Facebook Page. A Review tab does exactly what it says – it collates and publishes reviews written by your fans and visitors on your Facebook Page. There are many research reports that indicate the growing influence reviews by real users have on a buyer's confidence and decision to purchase. In addition, there is a school of thought that takes this idea further by saying that reviews by people they know and trust – i.e., their friends - carry more weight than reviews from strangers. Plus, nothing says "we value your feedback and comments" more than a tab that is dedicated to reviews about your products or services.

Legwork involved

If you want your Review tab to shine, there is some tough legwork to be done. But proceed with caution: if your Review tab is executed poorly, your brand reputation may suffer, so monitor your Review tab diligently.

Say for instance, you include a Review tab, but you don't get any reviews.

What can you do?

Perhaps a better way around this is to include a Review tab only after you actually have some reviews – and you are comfortable to share the content of the reviews on your Page – after all, didn't we say that your Facebook marketing efforts are to be carried out in small, incremental doses?

But what happens if you get many negative reviews?

What can you do?

The truth about review content is that it cannot be forced. Reviews are voluntary and subjective, and yes, it can get ugly. Do note that if you choose to intervene by weeding out the negatives, leaving behind just the over-glowing reviews, bear in mind that self-censorship can be picked up by your more discerning fans and backfire on you. We mentioned previously in Weapon #9 on Discussion Boards that one way to manage negative reviews is to publicize your policy regarding flaming comments or harassing behaviour. You might not be able to prevent negative reviews from happening, but the least you can do is to delete reviews that are baseless or spammy without any negative impact to your brand.

Like it or not, many businesses with Review tab Pages know that their reviews are the top three most viewed tabs. We guerrillas see it this way - publicity, whether it is good or bad, is still publicity. It gains you visibility, and puts you out there. The Facebook audience can be a discerning crowd. They watch to see how you are handling the publicity – be it positive or negative publicity, and they draw their own conclusions. If they like you, they would be converts to your cause, and customers for life. If they don't, well, they weren't really serious customers in the first place. The world of Facebook has some 955 million users. Surely we can carve our niche market out of that some 955+ million users, even if we choose to ignore or disassociate with some of them.

If all this talk about Reviews is making you feel too uncomfortable, remember that there are other ways to demonstrate your openness to feedback. For instance, you could occasionally share poll results instead of posting reviews. Polls are featured as Weapon #12 in this Chapter.

Our advice to you is, do what you are comfortable with and confident about; and not just because everybody is doing so. When you are authentic and sincere about the content on your Page, no one is any wiser if you had skipped or omitted the Review or Discussion Board tab.

Weapon #11: The Events Sharing and Invitations Tab

Events sharing and invitations are another arsenal in the range of Call-to-Action weapons – and we guerrillas love it. Many businesses have successfully pulled off Guerrilla Marketing events through the creative use of Event Sharing on Facebook, leveraging on the powerful word of mouth recommendation Facebook offers.

With Events Sharing, you can share details about an event you are organizing, say, a new promotion on your Facebook Page or Group. You could share maps, photos, contact information, and best of all, you can make use of guest management tools on Facebook to manage your event and invite fans and friends.

Up-coming events are displayed on the top right hand corner of your Home Page, and will continue to display on your list of invited friends until the function is disabled. Friends of friends who are also invited to the same event can see which friends will be attending the same event.

Different tools available for Pages and Groups

There are subtle but important differences in event invitations, depending on whether you have a Page or a Group.

Facebook differentiates between Pages and Groups by way of making certain tools available only for Pages and certain tools available only for Groups. If you are working from a Page, you can only invite fans to events that are posted on their News Feeds. We have previously highlighted that not all updates in News Feeds are picked up by fans, so this means that not all your fans might know of your event. If you are working from a Group, you get to send invites to the Group member's inboxes. There is a school of thought that believes that invites sent to a user's inbox stand a better chance of getting read.

But whether or not these differences could impact the response rate to your event is still moot. Events invites posted openly on your Page could be stumbled upon a visitor who may just bite and say yes to your event. Members who receive personal invites may still not bite if the event does not appeal to them in the first place. So play around and experiment to see what works best for your customers.

In Chapter 2, we talked about creating exclusivity for your Facebook fans as part of Rule #6 – Fans should not and cannot be treated equally. One of the best ways to introduce exclusivity is to organize exclusive Facebook events for your Facebook fans.

Take a minute to dream up the kind of guerrilla-type events you would hold with this weapon for your Facebook Fans:

What kind of events would you
organize for your Facebook Fans?

Now that you have dreamed up the kinds of possibilities you can organize on Facebook, you may wish to skip ahead to Weapon #17: Promotions app to help you get your event created and administered easily and quickly.

We couldn't help ourselves, so we have included some of our ideas for fan-exclusivity:

- Exclusive discounts for Facebook Fans
- By invitation only sales / previews
- Giveaways / freebies / free trials
- Samplers for new product launches
- Photo / video sharing contests
- Quizzes / puzzles
- Sweepstakes / lucky draws
- Web-based workshops / seminars
- Loyalty programmes

Not limited to Facebook

The beauty about Event Sharing on Facebook is that you can choose to extend your events beyond your Facebook Fans. For example, CozyCot.com, an online women's lifestyle portal, has successfully integrated their Facebook events with their online portal by not only featuring weekly giveaways for their Facebook Fans, but also promoting shopping spree events held on their web portal, effectively increasing their overall web presence.

Weapon #12: The Questions & Polls Tab

Facebook has a feature that you can use to ask questions on your Page. Responses to your questions are automatically reflected onto your Page. There is also a Facebook Poll app that enables you to conduct polls on your fans. The app comes with the option to publish results of your polls on your Page.

What type of questions to ask?

Posting open-ended questions and conducting polls can engage, and even entertain, your fans on Facebook in meaningful ways. It is a wonderful way to connect with your fans, and to win you new fans.

Here are two types of questions Guerrillas can post in polls:

1. <u>Cloud-Type Questions</u>: ask questions to help you make decisions about your business. For instance, you are in the middle of designing a new product, and you are considering new colors for your product. You could choose to apply a cloud strategy by asking your fans which colors would be more suitable for your product—hot fuschia or steel grey? - and let your fans help you decide. Everyone loves to feel helpful and that they have contributed to a good cause – they are more likely to come back for more. And you – you get instant feedback about what's hot and what's not.

2. <u>Provocative Questions</u>: ask questions that are provocative in nature—highly opinionated statements that will provoke more responses from your fans. For example, on a regular basis, administrators of Victoria's Secrets' Facebook Page ask highly-opinionated but fun questions that revolve around the idea of 'What is sexier'. One day it was, "What is sexier - legs or cleavage?" Another day it was, "What is sexier - candlelight dinner or breakfast in bed?" Simple, clean fun and extremely effective.

   Caution: guerrillas are respectful. In Chapter 1, one of the "guerrilla attitudes" highlighted was that guerrillas have an obligation to put money into their coffers, and not looks of horror or shock or disgust on the faces. Your fans are intelligent and discerning. Being provocative does not equate to being rude or disrespectful. If viewers do not get the respect they deserve from your Page, they will look for it elsewhere.

3. <u>Opinionated Questions</u>: Victoria's Secrets looks as though they have it easy because they sell sex, but questions need not always be provocative in order to evoke response. Some questions naturally solicit opposing opinions, camps or schools of thought. For instance, if you own an ice cream

store, you could ask questions like: which is a better topping: fruit or fudge? Can you see how you could plan marketing strategies based on your fan's responses?

Polls

Polls are a useful way of seeking reviews. They are more useful than open-ended comments or reviews because the responses can be controlled. Visitors to your Page can select from a range of pre-determined responses, and you can collate the results and share them as part of your content. There is a Poll app on Facebook that allows you to carry out marketing surveys in an easy manner – such as from the comfort of your cubby hole or bedroom, but it certainly does not lessen the hard work required by your task force to craft first-rate questions in the first place. That comes with any marketing campaign – guerrilla style or not.

Asking the right questions can open a mine field of data that can aid targeted marketing for your future marketing campaigns. For instance, you could close the gap between desire and purchase with greater accuracy as you learn more about your fans' preferences.

Ten-Hut! Weapon Tip #5:

Look for the Poll app by using Facebook's Search Function.

Weapon #13: The Photos and Videos Sharing Tab

Another element of Facebook to harness is its sharing nature. When you and your fans share information, you are making connections with one another. And it is this connection that deepens relationships. One of the main draws of Facebook is its sharing of photos and videos by users. According to Facebook, more than 250 million photos are uploaded each day in Facebook.

Who shares what?

So who shares, and what can you share about your business? Well, since you started the Page, it is only natural that you should share some information first.

The first thing to note about sharing is that it does not necessarily have to be new information. In fact, maintaining a consistent web identity – posting the same videos and photos online in different channels - can help you build your brand's awareness. So go ahead, share your current commercials, presentations, product photo shoots, and tutorial videos that are posted elsewhere on the web on your Facebook Pages – your website, your blog… just be careful not to overdo it.

Facebook has made it relatively easy to link up online content that you may have posted elsewhere. For instance, if you have videos posted on YouTube, the YouTube for Pages app allows you to link your videos from YouTube to your Facebook Page. If you have photos shared on Flikr, these can also be exported into your Facebook Pages quite easily.

> Maintaining a consistent web identity – posting the same videos and photos online in different places - can help you build your brand's awareness.

What if you have nothing to share?

If you don't have existing photos or videos, it's not the end of the battle. Guerrillas don't give up just because of this. You can still leverage on the power of your community to get a fair share of photos and videos going for your Pages. For example, on the Facebook Pages of ice-cream maker Ben & Jerry's and Starbucks respectively, are photos of happy fans enjoying their favourite ice cream / coffee from all over the world. Their Walls are filled with warm comments and feedback from happy customers, creating a sense of belonging to a warm, ice-cream / coffee-loving community. That is customer loyalty at its best.

Ten-Hut! Weapon Tip #6:

Not all Weapons need to be permanent features on your Page.

Events Sharing & Invitation (Weapon #11), Questions & Polls (Weapon #12) and Photos and Video Sharing (Weapon #13) can feature as part of your Wall activity instead of featuring as permanently separate Tabs on your Page if these are ad-hoc activities for your business.

Weapon #14: Facebook Marketplace

Like most other online tools, it was simply a matter of time before Facebook launched its own ecommerce facility. For Facebook, their answer was Facebook Marketplace, an online classifieds feature within the Facebook community.

The key difference between Facebook Classifieds and other traditional classifieds is the social element, hence the coining of a new phrase, "social commerce". What social commerce means is that you are not just buying or selling to people locally within your neighbourhood, you are buying or selling to people who know you, or you know them. This is because your friends who use Facebook's Marketplace are listed at a corner of Facebook's Marketplace Page.

Facebook Marketplace is useful for businesses that need to post new information about their products or services on a regular basis, such as real estate companies, recruitment agencies or used car dealers. Such businesses would be able to list their classifieds elsewhere within the Facebook community rather than cluttering up their Facebook Pages or Profiles.

Why would you consider listing on Facebook?
If your business relies on online classifieds, Facebook Marketplace could be an attractive option for you as the coverage of your classified listings is automatically linked to other social networking platforms such as Twitter, Oodle and MySpace. Unlike independent listings on online classifieds, listing on Facebook Marketplace also increases the authenticity of your listings, since each listing can be traced back to your Facebook Profile / Page. This in turn could also boost your overall Facebook presence.

Drawbacks
One drawback about Facebook Marketing is that the barrier to entry is set pretty high. For starters, listing your products or services on Facebook Marketplace isn't exactly the same as having your own personal place within Facebook for commercial transactions. If you do wish to add your Marketplace listings as one of your personal places within Facebook – the only way would be to include your listings on the Marketplace as a tab on your Facebook Page / Profile. But to do so means you need to subscribe as an Oodle Pro user – this is considered a "premium" service offered by Oodle – which essentially means you have to pay for the service.

Another drawback of Facebook Marketplace is that this is still a fairly new feature on Facebook. Recently introduced in 2007, Facebook Marketplace was then handed over to be developed by third-party developer, Oodle, and re-launched in 2009. Hence, in terms of usage, its popularity and outreach lags behind other more established online classified marketplaces such as eBay or Craig's List. At the time of writing, according to the official Facebook

Marketplace Page, there are more than 3 million monthly active users. While this number might be impressive in itself, its actual popularity among Facebook users remains fairly insignificant, when compared against the some 955 million current active Facebook users.

Despite its apparent drawbacks, we Guerrilla Marketers would not be so quick as to dismiss the potential Facebook Marketplace offers. Although on the surface, the classified section of Facebook might seem fairly limited in terms of marketing opportunities, it could turn out to be a very interesting tool to harness. For a start, we especially like the fact that Facebook Marketplace has the ability to reach out to other Facebook users (read: who are not your friends). If your goal was to boost your Facebook or online presence by drawing in more traffic to your business Profile / Page, this feature could just be the right weapon to use.

Ten-Hut! Weapon Tip #7:

Another way to integrate an ecommerce facility is to look for apps that help you set up a mini-store within your Facebook Page. For example, third-party developer North Social has a Show & Sell feature that permits Pages to incorporate an online retail store within a Facebook Page.

Weapon #15: Feed Burners

Creating a Facebook Page does not mean that you throw out your other web-based marketing resources such as existing websites, blogs or Twitter. Rather, we guerrillas would reinforce our business' online presence by linking our Facebook Pages to existing blogs, podcasts, videos or photo-sharing facilities. And, to make our job easier, we will look for apps that can help us in this respect. This is where Feed Burners apps come in.

Blog RSS, Facebook Twitter, RSS Graffiti

Feed Burner apps automatically connect "feeds" - content - from your other web-based sources and load them onto your Facebook Pages. For instance, you have a blog about your business. There is a Blog RSS Feed Burner that can link your blog to your Facebook Pages. If you have been using Twitter to disseminate product launches or special discounts, there is a Facebook Twitter app that can support your tweets neatly onto a corner of your Facebook Page. If you are an administrator of a Facebook Page, you may be interested in RSS Graffiti – this is an app that helps Page Administrators check feeds that Administrators read on partner websites, and post them as new entries on to the Facebook Pages they are administering. Social bookmarking website Digg is an example of one of the pioneer partner websites whose content can be fed onto Facebook News Feeds automatically.

The advantage of using Feed Burners is that this is essentially a covert exercise on generating automatic News Feeds for your fans, without you or your administrators having to load in independent status updates onto your Facebook Page that you have already done elsewhere, say on your blog or Twitter account. This can go a long way towards stretching your time spent on Facebook to achieve brand awareness on the web.

Weapon #16: Plug-ins

A Plug-in is a ready-made, standalone software feature that you can use to enhance your Page or elsewhere, for example, your external website or blog. With Plug-ins, you don't need to have special IT skills or knowledge to pull off a professional look for your website or Facebook Page – you simply need to know what's out there and what could work for you. Most Plug-ins are free to use.

In Facebook, the Call-to-Action buttons – for instance, the "Like" or "Recommend" buttons - are common social plug-ins that you can use to strengthen your Facebook presence and boost your overall online presence. Here are three plug-ins offered by Facebook that we like:

Visit Us on Facebook

On your corporate website or blog, you could include a banner or Facebook Badge, inviting visitors to your external website to visit you on Facebook to participate in events or entice your visitors to Facebook. This is a simple yet effective way to direct existing traffic from your corporate website or blog to your new Facebook Page.

Facepile

Facepile, or Facebook Fan Box, is a listing of photographs of your fans who have liked your Facebook Page that you can feature on your website or Page – it provides you and your readers with an idea of who your fans are, and who they connected with. When you do this, you are also saying something else very powerful. You are saying, 'I don't just have a fan base. I have a community of fans whom I can put names and faces to.' And that is a powerful statement. More about Managing Friends is covered in Weapon #24: Managing Friends and Fans.

LiveStream

LiveStream enables real-time sharing of videos and webinars on Facebook Pages. If the nature of your business or events involves real-time seminars / talks or live performances, this is the plug-in you want to have on your Page.

Difference between Plug-ins, Add-ons & Apps

The main difference lies in the scope or ability of the program. A plug-in is a simple, limited feature that you can include on a Page, for example, Facepile. It is a standalone, complete software program that can function by itself.

An add-on or extension, as the term suggests, requires existing and/ or compatible programs in order for it to work.

Of the three, apps are the most sophisticated in terms of programming and hence abilities and functions: think the ability to conduct polls or manage events.

Weapon #17: Promotions App

Guerrillas know that many Facebook users sign up to be a Friend or Fan of a business Page in the hope of receiving some benefit such as a freebie or special deal. Carrying out promotions is an effective way of increasing your fan base and generating further leads for your business. In the context of Facebook, promotions take on a slightly different twist that gets us guerrillas excited.

On Facebook, you can find apps that would help you quickly and easily create and administer promotions such as contests, sweepstakes, group deals and quizzes. What we especially like are apps that also have Facebook-friendly viral driver features, such as Friend Invites - inviting Friends to participate in share deals - or the Share Feature button - a pop-up dialogue box that asks users to post a message to their wall.

We have earlier pointed out that any status update on a user's Profile or Page is reflected on the News Feed page. If your fan posts a message to their wall, they are essentially helping you reach out to hundreds more who are on their list.

Promotions We Guerrillas Like:

Sign-Up Forms: usually in the form of a lightbox - a small window overlay that seeks basic contact information from the user but does not take the user away to another Page or website)

User-generated Contests (UGC): photo / essay contests are popular choices. Winners can be voted by the public or appointed jury to boost engagement

Coupon Giveaways

Group Deals / Deal Share: special discounts based on getting a certain number of users to commit to a purchase

Knowledge Trivia / Quizzes

Sweepstakes (giving away prizes based on random draws)

Examples of promotions apps providers

There are a number of promotions apps developed by third party developers to help you create and administer promotions easily. North Social and LiveWorld's Facebook CMS are examples of Facebook-based promotions apps you can use. When selecting which apps to use, bear in mind that some promotions apps work only in Facebook's interface, while other promotions apps, for example, Award-winning Wildfire, work from an external website, making it possible for you to integrate publicity events with other external websites , for instance, corporate websites or blogs.

Examples of promotions apps providers:

- North Social
- LiveWorld
- Wildfire

Weapon #18: Moderating Forums on Facebook

When you have a lively Discussion Board or forum, and a strong following by fans and visitors, you know that time is of essence in managing user-generated content on your Facebook Page. If you are unable to commit resources to manage this aspect of your Facebook Page, the next best course of action would be to look for some support to develop, operate, organize and moderate the user-generated content of your Facebook Page. One way is to outsource this function to professional social media programming agencies such as LiveWorld.

Introducing… LiveWorld

LiveWorld is a community programming agency that offers businesses unique products and services to ease the management of discussions and conversations in social media. Of particular interest to us guerrillas is LiveWorld's Facebook Forum introduced in 2010. LiveWorld's Facebook Forum is a conversation application that seamlessly integrates onto existing Facebook Pages to facilitate the conversations between a business and its fans (e.g. uploading of text, videos, and photos) as a standalone tab.

In addition, there are moderation tools businesses can use on the Discussion Board, such as the ability for moderators to set up multiple forums with unlimited topical threads, highlight topics, focus on top contributors or hot topics, post announcements, ask & answer questions, and even carry out polls without the need for additional or sophisticated programming skills.

In addition to products, LiveWorld also offers outsourced human moderator services to businesses – these professional moderators can be hired to review user content on Discussions Boards and Forums and take appropriate action to manage discussions based on pre-set guidelines. Reports are then generated for the business so that the business will know the active threads and feedback received. Depending on your needs, LiveWorld's Advanced Power Moderation Tools can vet up to 1,000 posts per hour on Facebook.

One of the criticisms often raised about Facebook is that not all business owners are "cut out" for Facebook, simply because they do not have the time or the personality to engage their fans, for example, they could be shy. Even if you do not think you have the personality for Facebook, you can still launch a successful Guerrilla Facebook Marketing campaign by engaging a third party to do the work for you. To this end, there are service providers such as LiveWorld who have a team of professionals who can be hired to carry out marketing campaigns on Facebook.

We guerrillas like LiveWorld's solutions. It comes with a price, but it is an option for businesses with a larger budget.

Weapon #19: Facebook Search

At first glance, this weapon might not appear to have any firepower. Why would anyone recommend this function as a Guerrilla Marketing weapon? But we guerrillas know better. There is a reason why Internet search engines like Google and Yahoo have grown into corporations of their own. In an information world, the search service is an indispensable tool.

Seek and Connect

The ubiquitous search function on Facebook is often times overlooked as a weapon in its own right.

A simple search function on Facebook can throw up plenty of opportunities for Guerrilla Marketers. Trust us: this is much better than cold-calling. For instance, we could search and make contact with relevant Facebook Groups or Fans who may be interested in our business. We could browse through our search results to decide on whom to invite to our events, or to view our Facebook Pages or to join our Groups and/or Group Discussions. If we have chosen our search parameters well, we are increasing the chances of increasing our fan base and growing our Facebook presence. Facebook's search function is also useful for finding out what apps are available to help you build or maintain your Facebook Page or Profile.

It doesn't get better than this. Really.

Weapon #20: Facebook Places

Facebook Places is a location-based service facility that identifies the geographical location of Facebook users by way of a check-in from using a mobile device, enabling Facebook users to indicate where they have been via Facebook. Facebook Places also helps users identify their friends who are located nearby to them in real-time, in addition to receiving local deals and discounts closest to the user's location.

Updating the buy loyal strategy

Facebook Places brings a new dimension to the age-old strategy, to buy local. Imagine the marketing possibilities that could be opened to you, if you knew that your fans were nearby your place of business. This feature literally takes on a new spin as it has the ability to bring fans to your shop front. How would you entice them to your shop front? What kind of location-based deals would you craft for fans who check-into a place listed on your Pages? Would you consider varying your discounts or deals by changing variables, such as coming in a group, or coming at a certain time to help your business grow?

> We guerrillas would want to correlate data on Facebook with other data such as sales or external website traffic statistics.

Weapon #21: Facebook Analytics

As a Guerrilla Facebook Marketer, how would you discern if your guerrilla attack has been victorious?

Welcome to the new face of market research, where being connected to your customers and knowing more about what your fans are doing on your Page are closely monitored in Facebook.

Want to know how active your Facebook presence has been? Curious to track your user interactions on your Facebook Pages and tabs?

No problem. There are features that can collate data such as the number of Likes, the number of daily active users, the number of new Fans, who is clicking on which tabs and on which ads, who has joined the Fan's list, and so on. We have one word for you: Analytics.

'Analytics' is the term used to describe data monitoring and analysis by applying operational research methodologies. It is a concept that has become commonplace for businesses and marketers alike when it comes to monitoring online activity on websites, blogs, social media and the like.

Information and analytics are the core businesses of Facebook. The analytic tool offered to users is known as Facebook Insights. Facebook Insights is a free analytic service available for all Facebook Pages. Some users of Facebook Insights have criticized its simplistic nature. If you feel that way, you are free to engage third-party analytics providers – there are others out there – e.g. Socialbakers' Analytics or Appdata.com.

The main crux of getting data is not data collation, but how we decode the data: what we do with the data we receive. We guerrillas treat analytical tools like report cards. Data can tell us what is working and what is not. Data can tell us what is helping us achieve our goals, and what is not. To answer that question, we need to first ask ourselves what we wanted to achieve from our Facebook marketing campaign in the first place – more on this in Chapter 6.

Facebook data we want to decode

If you are a Facebook Freshie, you might be wondering how you are connecting with your visitors. If so, data such as which Pages are viewed most frequently, how many Likes and how many comments you received per post, or the number of views per tab might be of interest to you. Or, you might be wondering if your content is relevant and appealing to your fans. If so, data such as number of unsubscribes and unLikes would tell you a lot about the appeal factor of your content to your current fans.

Data can also help us decide on how to tweak our Facebook activities. For instance, we may adjust our content or approach according to the demographic data such as gender or age on our fans in order to attract the kind of fans we are after. Or it could be as simple as adjusting when we post new content, based on the peak times for fan responses.

And we guerrillas are not just content with decoding simple data. We would want to take our decoding exercise further by, say for example, exporting the data into a simple excel sheet, and correlating this data with other data such as sales data or your external website traffic statistics. For instance, if you are giving out coupons on your Facebook Page, you can track activity to pinpoint how many Facebook Fans eventually make a purchase on your website or shop front using those coupons downloaded from Facebook. Or, you could correlate website traffic statistics to access if there has been any directed inbound

/ outgoing traffic between your external websites and Facebook and vice-versa.

Interested to find out more? Turn to Chapter 6 on Dollars and Cents: Making Sense of Guerrilla ROI where we discuss measuring outcomes in greater detail.

Weapon #22: Facebook Ads

Facebook Ads are the most blatant marketing tool available on Facebook for guerrilla marketers. Each ad is posted on the right column of a Page or Profile of Facebook users. If you Liked a particular ad, your preference will be noted and reflected thus for all your other friends to see. Facebook ads can drive traffic to external websites, or to another Facebook Page.

Facebook runs their advertising service as a self-service function: you are expected to do your own ad copy, and ad space is extremely limited. There are just 135 characters for the body of the ad - this means your ad copy text has to be absolutely watertight and, at the same time, look creatively eye-catching.

Facebook also offers advertisers the option of audience targeting. Which means, you, the advertiser, gets to control who gets to see your ads – you can specify the location of viewers as determined by IP addresses, age, educational status, gender, language and so on of your intended viewers. Incidentally, Facebook ads can also be targeted at people on their birthday.

Ten-Hut! Weapon Tip #8:

Ad Tips!

If you are a Facebook Freshie or new to Facebook ads, here are some tips to help you get the most out of your Facebook ads:

- CPC (cost-per-click) or CPM (cost-per-mille/thousand impressions)? On your first try, we say opt for CPC to keep your costs down simply because you don't pay for that version of that ad if you do not get any clicks on your ad.

- Spilt-test your ads. To spilt-test means to run your ad with one or two variables changed in order to assess which version of your ad is most effective.

- Ads with attractive images get clicked on more than those without images. So it pays to give some attention to your ad's image, no matter how small the image is.

- Complement your ad with a functional landing page that has an email capture function.

- Reward visitors who sign up to be on your emailing list or become a Fan of your Page with downloadable coupons or free gifts, samplings or free trial periods for your service to build up trust.

- Read and re-read Facebook's guidelines and best practices at www.facebook.com/adsmarketing. Their guidelines do change from time to time!

Weapon #23: Facebook Sponsored Stories

Every time a Facebook user clicks on the Like button, Facebook collects the information, and stores it in their great library of information for use later on. Facebook Sponsored Stories is one of them.

Facebook Sponsored Stories is a new ad format. It features customized friends/fans' actions that have been turned into ad message promotions that can be bought by businesses. Basically, it is a customized message based on your friends' / fans' actions.

Stories based on actions taken by fans/friends

Sponsored stories include actions captured by the Facebook Places function that checks-in fans or friends into businesses (Weapon #20: Facebook Places), Page posts and Page Likes (Weapon #7: Call-To-Action Buttons), RSVPing to an event and so on. How it works is that businesses can pay to feature a percentage of all check-ins to their businesses featured in a Facebook Sponsored Story slot on the right-side column of Facebook Pages and Profiles. The message of the story could go along the lines of '300 friends have checked into ABC business today', or 'x number of people or so [name of friend] and so [name of friend] liked this (ad)'.

From a Guerrilla Marketer's point of view, Facebook Sponsored Stories is an interesting concept to explore. Perhaps if guerrilla marketers know how to pacify Facebook users who have rallied against Facebook for selling their Likes, and not getting a share of the proceeds, this could turn out to be an even more powerful tool for businesses.

Weapon #24: Managing Friends and Fans

Any Guerrilla Marketer knows the importance of maintaining lists. Creating and maintaining a database is a tactical necessity for all Guerrilla Marketers. Facebook knows this too, and makes it easy for businesses to manage their lists without any cost.

Friends List

It matters not whether you have 100, 1,000 or 10,000 friends or fans. The principle of maintaining a Friends List on Facebook remains the same: your target is to build a relationship for each name on your list, one at a time. This isn't a popularity exercise; it is a Guerrilla Marketer's golden rule.

One useful way to help you connect and build relationships is to organize your lists into sub-lists according to interests, demographics, preferences, and so on. Facebook makes it easy for you with the Friends List function: you can have up to 1,000 friends on a maximum of 100 separate Friend Lists – so why not make full use of this feature? With organized Friends Lists, you can carry out targeted marketing campaigns by sending out specific content to specific groups of fans on your lists through invites and private messages. You can even determine who gets to read what content on their News Feeds.

If you have existing email lists you wish to import from other emailing systems, say in Yahoo or AOL, but not Gmail at this time of writing, you can do so by making use of the "Import Your Facebook Friends' Email Addresses" function on Facebook.

Ten-Hut! Weapon Tip #9:

Not all fans might share their friends list with you. There are privacy controls on Facebook that can limit access to information about your fan's friends who are more careful about sharing personal information.

What can you do?

Seek to get them interested first. Share compelling content about your business, encourage them to join events or group discussions. And always offer them the option of signing up to be your fan or friend.

Top Friends

Facebook has made it easier for Guerrilla Marketers to carry out targeted marketing campaigns by way of the Top Friends feature. Top Friends is a feature that helps you identify who are the top Friends or Fans to your Facebook Profile / Page. These are your friends / fans who have interacted with your Business Page recently, or the most. There is a neat Fanbox widget tool we featured as Facepile (Weapon #16: Plug-ins) that you can adopt to feature your friends/fans on your Facebook Page or elsewhere, but not in Facebook Groups.

When you have a growing list of Top Friends, you know that you are doing something right on Facebook. Good for you! Our advice to you is to treat your targeted marketing campaign for your Top Friends as a full-on assault. Continue to connect to them in regular conversations. Make them feel special – organize exclusive events for them, offer them special deals and treats. Get them to recommend you to their friends, or provide positive reviews and feedback to your Facebook Page.

Weapon #25: Facebook Connect

This is how Facebook goes beyond its Facebook interface to interact and grow its presence with the web community at large.

Third-party links

Facebook Connect is a facility that enables links between Facebook and third-party partner websites. These third-party partner websites have existing arrangements with Facebook that enable Facebook users to leave comments, Like or share with their friends as they would on Facebook Pages, or even to access their email accounts without having to log in again from external websites. At the time of writing, Facebook announced that they are "transitioning away from the Facebook Connect brand to reflect that there is one platform behind any integration with Facebook. This change has no impact for developers using Connect; everything is still part of Facebook Platform." The change in Facebook's direction suggest that Facebook no longer sees Facebook Connect as merely a weapon to be wielded; it has become part of Facebook's philosophy – in other words, it will become easier for businesses to make connections between their Facebook Pages and third party websites.

That aside, what can Facebook Connect offer to a Guerrilla Marketer now? Obviously, if you already have an existing website or blog, leverage on this tool to boost your online presence by directing traffic from your website or blog to your Facebook Page and vice-versa. As more connections and links are made between your Facebook Page and website or blog, you will also understand better how or what makes your fans connect to you online, or what makes them turn away from you. There's more on online influence in Chapter 7 - The Faceoff: Where do we go from here?

So that's all 25 weapons – dissected and discussed. Let's take a breather and review them again, this time, presented in an easy-on-the-eye table:

Table 3: At a Glance: Summary of Guerrilla Facebook Marketing Weapons

Weapon #1	**Facebook Page** Page vs. Profile?
Weapon #2	**The Wall** Information dissemination & publicity tool

Weapon #3	**News Feed**
	How little updating is too little? How much is too much?
	You don't get to control the News Feed function of your fans
	Not "new" information
Weapon #4	**Facebook Groups**
	Encouraging Group Discourse
	Group Vs Page
Weapon #5	**Facebook Fan Pages**
	Fan Pages deserve your attention
Weapon #6	**Facebook Apps**
	Facebook apps we guerrillas love
	App woes
Weapon #7	**The Call-to-Action Buttons**
	The Like Button
	The Become a Fan &Follow Us on Facebook Buttons
	The Comment or Share Buttons
	The Recommend Button
Weapon #8	**Customized Tabs**
	Static FBML

Weapon #9	**The Discussion Board** Discussion Boards vs. Groups Cutting both ways Managing Discussion Boards
Weapon #10	**The Review Tab** Legwork involved
Weapon #11	**The Events Sharing and Invitations Tab** Different tools available for Pages and Groups What kind of events can you organize for your Facebook Fans? Not limited to Facebook
Weapon #12	**The Questions and Polls Tab** What type of questions to ask? Polls
Weapon #13	**The Photos and Videos Sharing Tab** Who shares what? What if you have nothing to share?
Weapon #14	**Facebook Marketplace** Why would you consider listing on Facebook? Drawbacks
Weapon #15	**Feed Burners** Blog RSS, Facebook Twitter, RSS Graffiti

Weapon #16	**Plug-ins** Visit us on Facebook Facepile LiveStream
Weapon #17	**Promotions App** Promotions we guerrillas like Examples of promotions apps providers: North Social, LiveWorld, Wildfire
Weapon #18	**Moderating Forums on Facebook** Introducing… LiveWorld
Weapon #19	**Facebook Search** Seek and Connect
Weapon #20	**Facebook Places** Updating the buy local strategy
Weapon #21	**Facebook Analytics** Facebook data we want to decode
Weapon #22	**Facebook Ads** Ad Tips
Weapon #23	**Facebook Sponsored Stories** Stories based on actions taken by friends/fans

Weapon #24	**Managing Friends and Fans**
	Friends Lists
	Top Friends
Weapon #25	**Facebook Connect**
	Third party links

The reason why we guerrillas love Facebook as a marketing tool is because more than 20 of the 25 Facebook-specific weapons we have highlighted are free. This is exactly what we guerrillas mean by focusing on time, energy, imagination and information instead of big budgets.

Selecting Guerrilla Weapons

But wait—there is more. Other than just having a good understanding of Facebook guerrilla weapons, guerrillas also need to wield the right weapons at the right time. One way to help us choose the right weapons is to prioritize which weapons we would want to try first.

Take some time to go through the list below, and classify the weapons into the order of priority for your next Guerrilla Marketing campaign. For each weapon, ask yourself: is this weapon something I can implement straightaway? Or is this weapon something I can try next if Plan A does not work out? Or, is this weapon to be kept in cold store for this particular marketing campaign?

The Priority Exercise on the subsequent pages is designed such that it can be re-used over and over again. Before starting on the exercise, make a few copies now for multiple use later on. Trust us, you will need the blank copies for future use.

	Ten-Hut! Weapon Tip #10:

Ten-Hut! Weapon Tip #10:

If you are undecided on how to prioritize, you could also check out what your competitors or "neighbouring" businesses are doing.

Campaign Name: _____

Priority Exercise: Selecting Your Guerrilla Weapons

	Weapon	Implement straightaway	Next to try	Cold store
#1	**Facebook Page**			
#2	**The Wall**	ABSOLUTELY		
#3	**News Feed**	ABSOLUTELY		
#4	**Facebook Groups**			
#5	**Facebook Fan Pages**			
#6	**Facebook Apps**			
#7	**The Call-to-Action Buttons**			
	Like			
	Become a Fan			
	Follow Us on Facebook			
	Comment or Share			
	Recommend			
#8	**Customized Tabs**			
#9	**Discussion Board Tab**			
#10	**The Review Tab**			

#11	**Events Sharing and Invitations**			
	As a Tab?			
	As a Wall Activity?			
#12	**Questions and Polls**			
	As a Tab?			
	As a Wall Activity?			
#13	**Photos and Videos Sharing**			
	As a Tab?			
	As a Wall Activity?			
#14	**Facebook Marketplace**			
#15	**Feed Burners**			
	Blog RSS			
	Facebook Twitter			
	RSS Graffiti			
	Others?			
#16	**Plug-ins**			
	Visit us on Facebook			
	Facepile			
	LiveStream			
#17	**Promotions App**			
#18	**Moderating Forums on Facebook**			
#19	**Facebook Search**			
#20	**Facebook Places**			
#21	**Facebook Analytics**			
#22	**Facebook Ads**			
#23	**Facebook Sponsored Stories**			

#24	**Managing Friends and Fans**			
	Friends Lists			
	Top Friends			
#25	**Facebook Connect**			

CHAPTER 5

COMMENCE BATTLE PLAN

Before a battle commences, guerrillas must first plan for one.

Guerrillas believe in having a battle plan. Having a plan simplifies your marketing campaign. It makes things easier. It helps you get from Point A to Point B. It puts what you need to do into perspective, and highlights what you need to focus on. It helps eliminate emergencies and non-important activities, so that you can reap maximum gain from minimum stress while you are at it.

Seven Elements for a Seven-Sentence Guerrilla marketing plan

Guerrilla Marketing is not something that happens overnight, but the decision to become a Guerrilla Marketer can be done in an instant. And once that decision is made, the next step is to put that decision into words: a plan. For guerrillas, a marketing plan has seven elements:

Seven elements for a Seven-Sentence Guerrilla Marketing Plan:

(1) Purpose

(2) Benefits

(3) Target market

(4) Weapons

(5) Niche

(6) Identity

(7) Projected budget

The first sentence focuses on the **purpose** of your Facebook marketing campaign. What do you want to achieve from your Facebook marketing campaign? What action do you want your customer to take? Do you want them to visit or re-visit your Facebook Page? Do you want them to become a fan of your Page? Do you want them to connect with you on your Page? Do you want them to participate in your events and polls? The purpose of your campaign needs to be measurable. For example, if you want to increase your fan base, what is that number you are looking at? 100 fans per week? 1,000 fans per week?

The second statement focuses on the **benefits** you want to stress to your Facebook audience to achieve your purpose set out in the first sentence. You want to be talking about them, not you, your business or your special offers. People want to talk about themselves – that is why they log on to Facebook. When you know what your fans want, you would be able to define what you have to offer them. When you can achieve this, your fans won't see you as selling them something they don't want – they will see you as someone who is helping them. That's how you build relationships with your customers. Guerrillas also know that less is more: focus on primary benefits: stressing one or two relevant benefits is more powerful than listing 50 benefits that don't mean much to your fans.

The third statement focuses on your **target market**. It is easy to market once you know exactly who to market to. Targeting involves determining who, when, where and why customers buy your product or service. Guerrillas believe in serving only what they serve best to those who want it. To do this, analyse the profiles of your existing fans, or existing followers of your blogs or websites. What are they like? Where are they from? When do they visit your blog or website? Guerrillas also like flexibility: they choose to have different target markets, and make different plans accordingly, depending on the needs of the target market.

The fourth statement focuses on what **weapons** you are going to use. A good Guerrilla Marketing Plan will almost always choose a combination of marketing weapons and ammo for maximum effect. And why not, since most of the weapons identified won't cause a dent in your marketing budget, but rather your imagination, time and energy. Going back to the exercise at the end of Chapter 4, and re-use the exercise sheet to identify specific weapons you want to use for each new marketing campaign you plan for.

The fifth statement focuses on your **niche** in Facebook. Your niche refers to your positioning in the marketplace – what your brand stands for. Some marketing experts refer to this as your unique selling point. When people come across your brand on Facebook, what is the first thing that pops into their head about your brand? What is the one thing you want visitors to your Page and fans to remember about your Page? With all the noise going on in Facebook, you really need to stand out. Your Page is not the only show in town.

The sixth statement is about your **identity** - who you are. This is not the public's image or perception of you – this is who you really are. Guerrillas don't believe in propagating perceived public images. Instead, they focus on being honest and direct about their identities. On Facebook, honesty really matters. Honesty is about being consistent. If you intend to connect with your fans on Facebook via ongoing authentic conversations, who you are will eventually show in the long run. Your fans will know what's real and what is not.

The seventh statement is putting money into your **marketing budget** to walk the talk when the need arises. Your marketing budget is expressed as a percentage of your gross sales, before deductibles.

Guerrillas aim to create a marketing plan that is brief, to the point, and written in simple, easy to understand language. Ideally, the length of the marketing plan should not exceed one page, and the plan, once completed, should be visible for all stakeholders to see and make reference to.

Now turn over to the next page to write out your Seven-Sentence Guerrilla Facebook Marketing Plan now.

Our Seven-Sentence Guerrilla Facebook Marketing Plan

1. The **purpose** of our Facebook marketing campaign is to _____

    _____

    _____

    _____ .

2. The primary **benefits** we want to stress are _____

    _____

    _____

    _____ .

3. Our **target market** is _____

    _____

    _____

    _____

4. The Facebook marketing **weapons** we will use include

    _____

    _____

    _____ .

5. Our **niche** position in the market is _____

    _____

    _____

    _____ .

6. Our **identity** is _____

    _____

    _____

    _____ .

7. Our marketing **budget** will be _____% of our gross sales.

    Date:

    Review Date:

    Next Review Date:

Action is the purpose of planning

It might take less than half an hour to write out a marketing plan, but writing is just the easy part.

The purpose of planning is action.

Even with the best of plans, guerrillas know that they can lose their way. They could start out inspired with the best of intentions, and raring to go, but lose steam along the way when things don't always go the way they planned it to. Or, when something unexpected crops up and cause the campaign to derail, they stop, turn back, or give up.

Without a certain level of conscious effort to be committed to any plan of action, it is almost impossible for any plan to be implemented successfully over a period of time. This is the reality of undertaking any new project. Guerrillas know that they have to work doubly hard to implement the plan, especially so when the initial results look dismal and disappointing. They know that if they commit to their well-conceived plan, they will see results.

This is why guerrillas recognize the need to review their marketing plans on a regular basis. To review means to take stock of what has happened since the implementation. Guerrillas will want to know what is working and what is not, and the earlier they know this, the better. A brief review could be carried out once every four to six weeks, followed by a more thorough review, say once every six to 12 months.

A battle plan should not change course once it is set in motion. Guerrillas will try to stick to their marketing plan for at least six months to a year without having to make major changes to their plans. For instance, the **purpose**, the primary **benefits**, and the **identity** of a plan are elements that should not be changed easily. However, there are times when change is necessary. For instance, the choice of **weapons** could change. A guerrilla might choose to drop from twenty weapons to just focus on five weapons that have consistently produced results, or the marketing **budget** could be adjusted as sale volumes increased.

Guerrillas don't change their plans just because they have changed their minds. Instead, they change their plans because they are compelled to do so. For instance, a new product that makes their product obsolete has been launched into the market. That kind of circumstance calls for drastic action.

How do you know if you have the perfect plan that is working best for you?

You will know it. You will know it because you are no longer making changes to your plan. You are simply doing what you have set out to do. And the more you do it, the better you become. And you enjoy it. When this happens, positive results always follow.

All guerrillas implement a marketing plan together with a marketing calendar.

Guerrilla Marketing Calendar

When it comes to calendars and the concept of time, guerrillas observe two rules:

1. If guerrillas don't make the time for it, they won't have time for it.
2. If guerrillas don't take control of their time, someone – or something – will fill up their calendar for them.

A marketing calendar goes hand-in-hand with a marketing plan. While a plan simplifies your marketing campaign, a calendar chronologizes your plan, literally, putting a time to each action you set out to do in your plan. Guerrillas love calendars. It breaks down the seemingly impossible into simple, bite-size portions by providing a sequence to guide you into taking on one task at a time. It also helps you keep an eye on all the other ongoing efforts and activities – it makes coordination easier. Finally, calendars establish a structured routine for guerrillas. When things start to fall apart, discipline steps in to take over, helping guerrillas stay on course.

Every guerrilla's calendar will look different. Hour-to-hour calendar formats are ideal for campaigns with very tight deadlines, while day-to-day calendar formats are useful for campaigns that need to be monitored on a daily basis. A week-by-week calendar format that drills down to daily tasks provides more flexibility than day-to-day or hour-to-hour formats. This format is useful when you are juggling a number of daily campaigns and tasks at the same time but also want control over your weekly schedule. A month-by-month calendar format is best reserved for on-going campaigns that have proven successful and require less review and supervision.

How do you get started? We first start by identifying the **key events in your industry** that could have an impact on your campaign. Think of events that gather together large groups of prospects or similar businesses. For example: trade shows, annual sales periods, competitions or awards, industry-wide seminars or conferences. When identifying these events, guerrillas would also think about how these events could be possible publicity opportunities for their marketing campaign as well.

Next, we list down the **key dates that are specific to your business**. For example, business opening anniversaries, new product season launches, dates for new store openings, annual sale periods, etc. This helps you plan ahead to avoid crowding of activities. For instance, you might want to re-think postponing the new product launch if it coincides with the day you are relocating. It also helps you fill in activities such that there are no excessive "lull" periods.

You want to keep a moderate but comfortable pace, and not be on sprint or dragging feet mode the entire period.

The next task is to **estimate how much time is needed** to complete each initiative or action listed in the plan. This could be expressed in hours, days, weeks or even months. It is not an easy task to estimate how much time is needed. It requires a lot of understanding of the process behind the task in order to be able to set realistic expectations. Guerrillas know that having "realistic" expectations is not the same as having "low" or "mediocre" expectations. Having realistic expectations is merely showing respect for the time it takes for something to blossom. Patience is a time-honored guerrilla attitude, as highlighted in Chapter 1 of this book.

To do this estimation systematically, our advice is to go back to the Priority Exercise on Selecting Your Guerrilla Weapons in Chapter 4. By this time, we have assumed that you have already chosen the weapons you want to use for this particular marketing campaign you have planned for. Refer to that same list to estimate how much time you will need per weapon that is to be implemented straightaway, and when you would want to implement it. For example, to conduct a poll on your Facebook Page once a month, you will need to set aside two hours of preparation time for it.

Next, include in your calendar, the **review dates** of your marketing plan. Highlight these dates. These are like your checkpoints - this is the time you get a report card for the work you have done.

Now you are almost there. Wait – we meant now you have finished reading this Chapter. Here's what you need to do now. On the following page, we have designed a simple form for you to fill up all those little details that we talked about. Once you have finished that, take out your favorite calendar format, and start filling in your calendar today.

Ten-Hut! Calendar Tip:

The reason why we don't have a calendar for you is because there are many beautifully designed calendar templates available today - and many are for free!

Word processing programs usually have a template for calendars, but don't limit yourself to that. If you intend to share this calendar with your staff, there are calendar programs that permit date or calendar sharing, or permit multi-format use - from emails to mobile phones to different web-based programs.

Find a pretty one that works best for you. If we had to look at something all the time, it might as well be pretty to look at, don't you agree?

Our Guerrilla Facebook Marketing Calendar

Campaign Date: from _____ to _____

1. Key industry events that will occur during the period of your campaign

2. Key dates for your business

3. Review dates

Chapter 6

DOLLARS AND CENTS: MAKING SENSE OF GUERRILLA ROI

No campaign starts off perfect

Guerrillas know that their campaign is not perfect when first launched. That is the natural order of things: it is to be expected. No one is perfect and certainly no one is expected to craft the perfect plan at the onset. But guerrillas know that a campaign can be perfected during the process.

This is why when guerrillas launch an attack, they do so in waves. They start with Strike One, pause, assess the damage and their position. After their assessment, they launch Strike Two, assess damage, pause to assess current position, then Strike Three... you get the picture. For every strike they make, they want to know if they gained any ground. They want to know which deployed weapons hit the target, and which ones did not. With that insight, they tweak their campaign – they could change weapons, tactics or timing. This is how they perfect their campaign – right there on the battlefield.

The same goes for your Guerrilla Facebook Marketing campaign. After you have finished reading this book, selected your Facebook weapons and drawn up your battle plan and calendar, you are set to go. In-between attacks, you would keep an eye on the effects of your campaign to assess how each weapon you have deployed is faring, and tweak your marketing campaign.

This is what we set out to do in this Chapter. To perfect our marketing plan, we need to learn ways to keep track of what we do.

Link efforts back to profits

When monitoring your Facebook marketing activities, be wary of the misconception that to keep track means to keep an eye of the indicators that we are trying to impact – be it number of fans, or Page Views, or directing traffic. While this kind of information is important, it is not enough.

Guerrillas want know how what they do affect their business' net profits. At the end of the day, being immensely popular on Facebook isn't enough. Having hundreds or thousands of fans is not going to pay bills. If a guerrilla had spent money on a Facebook ad, s/he will want to know, for that amount of money s/he spent, how many clicks it generated and how many impressions s/he got. That's part one. Guerrillas will also want to know how these clicks and impressions converted visitors into fans, and fans into buying (and paying) customers, preferably repeat customers.

This is the objective of guerrilla ROI - Return On Investment. Just like the guerrillas view that marketing is not just limited to the marketing department, guerrilla ROI is not just about monitoring the first ripple effects of a campaign. For it to be guerrilla-like, guerrillas always have the drive to find ways to link efforts back to profits.

And herein lie some contradictions: in Guerrilla Facebook Marketing, more time, energy and imagination is invested than actual money. It is not always easy to put a value to time or energy. Furthermore, since Facebook is a social tool – you could develop strong customer loyalty and improve your brand awareness, and these outcomes are not easily directly linked back to sales or net profits. So how can one put meaningful values to such investments?

There are two simple strategies we can apply to help clarify the link between our efforts and profits:

1. Think measurability

    Thinking in terms of measurability can help us perfect our plan.

    Say for instance, you are running a campaign to increase the number of overseas Facebook fans. You begin with a statement like 'with a marketing budget of $X, I will be able to increase the number of overseas Facebook fans by 100% from 1,000 to 2,000 in 8 weeks.'

    Can you see how powerful this statement is in advancing your marketing campaign?

    (Authors note: it might be a good idea to revisit what you had indicated as the purpose of your Guerrilla Facebook Marketing Plan in Chapter 5.)

    But that's not all. There is always more.

    Part two of your ROI exercise is to place a value on the outcome of your success. For example, 'we used to spend $A to reach out to overseas customers using ABC methods. Now on Facebook, it cost us $B. Our cost-savings is $C, and our overseas sales have increased to $D. Our ROI on overseas marketing expenses have improved by E times.'

Can you see how links are to be made back to profits?

2. Reflect the true meaning of ROI

Change the way you look at ROI. When you drill down the meaning of ROI, you will find many ways to measure ROI variables such as cost-savings, net results, saved man-hours, decreased spending, increased sales, and so on.

For instance, due to increased brand awareness on Facebook, your HR department no longer needs to spend on job placement advertisements to get a decent pool of better qualified candidates. This results in a cost savings of some $X per advertisement posting. Or you no longer spend money paying people to conduct market surveys to find out what your customers want, which used to eat up some $Y of your marketing budget. Now, you can do it for free on Facebook.

Stop, deliberate, and take note of the ideas that are running through your head as you consider the potential of thinking in terms of measurability, cost-savings, net results, saved man-hours, decreased spending and increased sales. Jot them down here:

_____

_____

_____

_____

_____

_____

_____

_____

Do you see some clarity as to how ROI can be approached in guerrilla Facebook ROI? Yes, skip ahead to the next section. No? Read on.

This is where we are going to give you the hard line: if, even after trying out the techniques we have suggested here, you still cannot find ways to link your efforts back to profits, consider this: it is possible that those efforts might not be worth pursuing in the first place. Guerrillas never forget that marketing is a business – if it is not going to show a profit, it is not guerrilla marketing.

When you find yourself in such a situation, clear your mind, and re-think your intended guerrilla marketing efforts once more. There are plenty of weapon combinations you can try. This might mean you will have to re-look Chapters 4 (Guerrilla Marketing Weapons) and 5 (Commence Battle Plan) once more, but it will save you a great deal of heartache later on.

Insights from Facebook

20 years ago, concepts like data analysis, data mining and data collation were delegated to the nondescript statistics department – something that management browses when "there is time". Today, information in the form of organized data is regarded as central to one's business strategy. Information is not only a decision-making tool, it has also become a commodity: Facebook has shown the world that a business empire can be based on the monetization of information. Since Facebook's inception, Facebook has shown the world that it does an excellent job of collating and using data than most other organizations and businesses in the world today.

In Facebook's world, we cannot talk about data without mention of Facebook Insights: Facebook's answer to data analytics. The data in Facebook Insights is viewed on its dashboard, accessible by logging in to one's Facebook account. It is presented in graphical format and users can choose to view data according to different variables. Facebook Insights is a secure page, and permissions to view the data metrics can be controlled by the Page administers. There's more background on Facebook Insights as a weapon in Chapter 4 (Weapon #21 – Facebook Analytics).

What Facebook Insights offers:

- # of interactions this week (# of Likes, comments, Wall posts)
- # of Active Fans this week, # compared to last week; total fans, # compared to last week
- Demographics (gender, age breakdown, %)
- Top countries, top cities, top languages
- Total fans vs total unsubscribed fans over time; new fans / removed fans
- Page Views

Stop, deliberate, and take note of the ideas that are running through your head as you think about the potential for generating all kinds of measurements, indicators and correlations you need. Jot them down here:

_____

_____

_____

_____

_____

_____

Techniques to help you keep track

Since Facebook has made it fairly easy for guerrillas to obtain traffic and activity data, guerrillas can focus more time, energy and attention in honing data analysis techniques to help them keep track of performance.

---

6 Basic Data Analysis Techniques to Master:

1. Ask questions
2. Preparation
3. Data collection
4. Organize data
5. Make associations or connections
6. Data Visualization

---

1. Ask Questions

   The basis of your data inquiry is based on what you want to know.

   For instance, you want to know how often you should update your Facebook Page (your question) in order to increase your Page Views (your purpose). To answer your question, you set up a hypothesis. A hypothesis is a statement based on assumptions or fact. In this case, you assume that you need to update everyday in order to get more Page views. You also assume that new content will boost Page views. Based on your hypothesis, you would identify indicators that will help you test your hypothesis. For example, indicators such as days of a week and/or hours of the day, Page Views.

Ten Hut! ROI Tip #1:

Asking specific questions can go a long way in determining the scope of your monitoring efforts. Since we are talking about guerrilla marketing here, focus your questions around the purpose of your guerrilla Facebook marketing campaign.

2. Preparation

Preparation is what you do before launching your campaign. Focus on actions that will help you test your hypothesis. Going back to our example of wanting to know how often you should update your Facebook Page in order to increase your Page views, what you can subsequently do is to post an update everyday for a week, and then not post any updates for a week in order to create a pool of data for you to analyse. Depending on how rigorous you want your testing to be, you could choose to perform this same action over a period of time, say 3 or 12 months, keeping to the same variables.

Ten Hut! ROI Tip #2

Have a good grasp of your current situation before starting on any campaign. This is important in establishing a baseline for comparisons later on – the before and after scenarios. The more observations you make now about your current situation, the clearer it will be for you when you make comparisons later on.

3. Data collection

Data collection refers to how we look for the information we need in order to do our assessment.

If you are a seasoned marketer, you will be relieved to note that the days of eye-boggling, back-breaking, time-consuming manual data collation and tracking are over, thanks in no small part to automated software for data analytics. Facebook's godsend to guerrillas is Facebook Insights. Although it is a godsend, it is not the only analytics tool. There were other analytics tools that we highlighted in Weapon #21- Facebook Analytics in Chapter 4 of this book.

Ten Hut! ROI Tip #3:

While analytical tools such as Facebook Insights can help us get the basic data we need, don't overlook other forms of data collection, such as the collection of downloaded discount coupons from Facebook at your store, or by simply asking new customers or fans where they first heard of your business. Such information can help you gain additional qualitative insights, especially when you are making associations and connections.

---

4. Organize data

Here, what we mean is how you sort out your data according to variables such as time (hourly, daily, weekly, monthly) or demographics (gender, age, location). We sort data in order to spot trends or patterns. For example, to answer the question, how often to update a Page, we could gain insight into when we should update, based on which hour of the day has the most Page Views, or which days of the month have the most Page Views. If you are using Facebook Insights, this sorting is already done for you – you can select to view your data accordingly. You can also export your data to your own database in the form of an Excel (.xls) or (.csv) file.

This step is necessary even though you have identified indicators for your data collection. This is because we do not operate in a vacuum: sometimes, we can get other insights when organizing the data collected. This is natural and part of the testing process.

Data organization also involves explaining data anomalies. ROI can be a pretty modest measuring tool: don't dismiss small numbers. These anomalies can actually turn out to be little nuggets of valuable information. For example, there could be a sudden rise in Page Views on public holidays, where people have more time to log in to their Facebook accounts to connect with others. This means if you plan ahead to post interesting content or events just before or on a public holiday, this might garner you new visitors to your Page.

Ten Hut! ROI Tip #4:

You don't have to invest in expensive data analysis tools to organize data. If you use Microsoft Office, the Excel program works well; if you use Apple's iWork, it's the Numbers program; or if you prefer OpenOffice, use the Spreadsheet function.

5. Make associations or connections

Making associations or connections means to cross reference the data collated with other factors in order to draw meaningful conclusions.

Making associations is an important step towards making sense of your guerrilla ROI. For instance, when your Page has significantly less Page Visits than Page views, it usually indicates that there is insufficient knowledge about your Page by visitors of fans, but those who have found your Page have found your content engaging.

Oftentimes, to make associations, we revert back to asking questions and drawing up more hypotheses. To answer our example of wanting to know how often you should update your Facebook Page in order to increase your Page Views, we would typically explore questions such as, 'How many new fans are there on days when new content is posted' and compare with 'How many new fans are there are on days when no new content is posted?'

Making comparisons generally refer to before and after situations, or making comparisons between two mediums – for example, your Facebook Page vs. your website. For instance, how does my $1,000 investment in Facebook marketing compare to my $1,000 investment in Google or Yahoo marketing?

Ten Hut! ROI Tip #5:

Associations and connections can also be made by applying simple mathematical formulae, such as ratios. For instance, Page Views / Wall Posts, or percentages - % of Page Views by fans / % of Page Views by visitors.

6. Data visualization

Data visualisation is a technique commonly used in data monitoring to pick out patterns and trends. Visualisation also aids communication, particularly in reports for management, bankers or investors. Bar and pie charts, histograms and scatter plots are the common forms of data visualization. Most, if not all data analytic software today present data that is already in some form of visualization. To drill down data further, Microsoft's Office Excel, Apple's iWork's Numbers and OpenOffice's Spreadsheet are equally capable of creating meaningful visuals. Visualization is also useful in drawing out connections and associations between variables.

Ten Hut! ROI Tip #6:

Playing with different combinations of variables and in different visualization forms with the same set of data can sometimes provide you with different and new perspectives.

By now, you would be raring to launch your marketing attack.

Before we end this Chapter, we leave you with something from Shane Gibson, author of Guerrilla Social Media Marketing, who raised an interesting insight about the guerrilla conundrum: guerrillas measure success in terms of net profits, but those profits are generated by intentional relationship-building strategies such as providing advice or helping to build trust with their fans. Since this is so, it is important for businesses to have a conscience based on the truth. What drives your intention to connect with your fans –

be it in the form of a poll, question, event or status update - must be sincere and true to you and what your business stand for. If you don't know the intention of what you are doing on Facebook, our advice is to go find it first. It won't work any other way.

Chapter 6: Dollars and Cents: Making Sense of Guerrilla ROI

1. No campaign starts off perfect
2. Link efforts back to profits – think measurability and reflect the true meaning of ROI
3. Six techniques to help you keep track:
    (1) Ask questions
    (2) Preparation
    (3) Data collection
    (4) Organize data
    (5) Make associations or connections
    (6) Data Visualization

CHAPTER 7

THE FACEOFF: WHERE DO WE GO FROM HERE?

ow you are ready to fly.

If you have followed from Chapter 1 to this far, you would have selected your weapons (Chapter 4), drawn out your Seven Sentence Guerrilla Facebook Marketing Plan and Calendar (Chapter 5), launched one or two attacks, and are keeping track of your performance (Chapter 6). Perhaps the initial results aren't exactly spellbinding, but patience is a guerrilla virtue. It will take some time for results to show. The important thing is, you have started on your journey.

The next steps will be very exciting times for you. Your Guerrilla Facebook Marketing journey is like a process – it has a beginning and a middle, but it doesn't have an end – unless of course, you call the shots to end it.

Once you begin on your journey, you will discover that this journey will be peppered with ups and downs. There will be challenges – some foreseen, others unforeseen. This journey, like life, as we know it, was never meant to be days filled with blue skies with flower-strewn paths. There will be grey skies and potholes along the way, but that only makes the journey more interesting. The longer you stay on this journey, the more adept you become at managing challenges that come your way to test your boundaries.

Moving beyond your Facebook backyard

Once you have grasped the mechanics of running a successful Facebook marketing campaign, you will start to explore the possibility of moving beyond your Facebook backyard. And when you do so, you will soon discover that while you can't deny or ignore Facebook, neither is Facebook the end all for your web-based marketing campaigns. So as you get better, how do you reach out to the next level? What other web-based mediums are there for you to explore?

How can you move beyond your Facebook backyard to grow your online influence as a whole? Does your business come up on the first page of main web search engines such as Google and Yahoo?

There is less magic and telepathy involved in putting out your online influence than you think. A guerrilla's online influence typically consists of a combination of different online platforms in order to drive web traffic to and fro your Facebook Page and other platforms. Facebook does not operate in a vacuum, and neither should your business. The web community has many websites which you can connect with in order to grow your online influence. For example, you could get listed on social book marketing sites, or participate in independent forum sites, contributing as experts or as advisors in your area of expertise or industry experience. Here are some websites that we have shortlisted that could provide you with some potential opportunities to expand your online influence:

Sites	Main Function	Your Thoughts?
Social Bookmarking sites (e.g. Digg.com and del. icio.us)	Visitors tag, share and rate their favourite Internet links	
User-generated Content sites (e.g. YouTube, Flickr.com)	Users upload media content (videos for YouTube and photographs for Flickr.com)	
Wiki-like sites (e.g. Wikipedia)	Users collaborate to create and edit content in a wide variety of topics	
Review sites (e.g. Epinions.com, Yelp)	Consumers share reviews about businesses, products or services	
Forum sites (e.g. Moneysavingexpert.com, RedFlagDeals)	Members hold discussions and conversations on a wide range of topics	

What about website traffic? How can you direct traffic from your existing website to your Facebook Page, and vice-versa?

Even Facebook itself recognized the need for its platform to be embedded within the larger web community. The evidence is in the creation of tools such as Facebook Connect (Weapon #25 in Chapter 4), Feed Burners (Blog RSS, Facebook Twitter, RSS Graffiti - Weapon #15) and Plug-ins (Visit Us on Facebook, Facepile, LiveStream - Weapon #16) that can help users connect within the wider web community. What about getting visitors to your website and/or Facebook Page to subscribe to your mailing list? Can you find a combination that best suits your business and the amount of energy and time you are willing to spend on boosting your online influence?

Going beyond the web

More and more people are turning to the Internet to get the scoop or story about businesses and brands. Although we say "more and more", it does not mean that everybody is on the web. In the year 2011, the world's population will cross over the 7 billion mark. But as of March 2011, out of the 7 billion people, only 2 billion are Internet users. Despite rapid technological advances, the world's Internet penetration rate averages at just 30.2% (www. internetworldstats), about 3 in every 10 people in the world are Internet users.

What's beyond the web? The real world – the one we live in, the one with some 5 billion people who are not Internet users, and who will demand and need products and services? How are you marketing your products and services to them?

Have you integrated your online marketing campaigns with your offline marketing campaigns? What do your printed pamphlets and brochures, your invoices and receipts, and your name cards say about your online presence? Is your Facebook Page prominently displayed on them? What about your shop front? Are there efforts to entice walk-in customers to log onto your online presence?

Are your offline systems compatible with your online systems? Can your customers make purchases easily online and pick up their purchases from your shop front? Is it easy for your customers and prospects to find your offline presence from your online presence? At the same time, are your walk-in customers to your shop front enticed to go online to look for your online presence?

Jot down some ways to integrate your online presence with your offline presence:

_____

_____

_____

_____

_____

_____

Changing Times

We are witnessing the dawn of the social media revolution.

We live in changing times.

In Chapter 1, we highlighted the Changing Face of Facebook. Facebook is in a constant state of change – they change policies, guidelines, and the way features are presented on the Facebook interface. Sometimes, they are announcements, other times, changes are just rolled out and users are expected to go with the flow. Some changes can have significant impact on businesses. For instance, to-date, the number of Facebook mobile users has increased to almost 200 million users. Facebook mobile users access their Facebook accounts while they are out and about from their mobile devices. Can you see the potential Facebook mobile can have for your business?

In addition to changes within Facebook, technologies that support social media have also evolved quickly. Technology not only moves fast. It has made things easier and simpler to accomplish. Thanks to new software technologies, guerrillas today can create Facebook Pages and websites competently and professionally by themselves, at a fraction of the cost, or even for free, with a little DIY. The greatest challenge is not dealing with technological change and computers, but the people behind the computers. Technology is only as good as the user. If you are not investing time and energy to learn more about software apps and changes in technology in general, you are missing out on this century's greatest invention.

Change and evolution.

This is the future of Guerrilla Marketing.

Are you growing yourself as your Facebook presence grows, in tandem with Facebook's growth?

ABOUT THE AUTHORS

Jay Conrad Levinson, father of Guerrilla Marketing, is the author of Guerrilla Marketing, a popular marketing book published in 1984 that remains the best-selling marketing book with more than 21 million copies sold world-wide. The Guerrilla Marketing book series today consists of 58 books available in 62 languages. Jay coined the term, "Guerrilla Marketing" while he taught marketing at the extension division of the University of California in Berkeley, a teaching position he did for a decade. Today, Guerrilla Marketing principles frequently appear as recommended readings for many MBA marketing programs. Jay has contributed a number of articles on Guerrilla Marketing to business magazines such as the *Entrepreneur* and *Inc.*, as well as for online columns as such *America Online, Fortune Small Business, Hewlett-Packard, Microsoft* and *Netscape.* Some notable marketing campaigns Jay collaborated on include the Jolly Green Giant and United's Friendly's Skies. As the Chairman of Guerrilla Marketing International, the marketing partner of Adobe and Apple, Jay is frequently invited to speak about Guerrilla Marketing at universities, professional organizations and corporations around the world. He has also sat on the Board of Leo Burnett Advertising, the Small Business Board of 3Com and Microsoft Small Business Council.

Kelvin Lim is an expert in human dynamics and motivation – he has been coaching, consulting, training and marketing since 1995. He is the first Guerrilla Marketing Certified Master Trainer in Singapore to be trained by Jay Conrad Levinson. He is also the principle consultant and CEO of Guerrilla Marketing Consulting, an organization that teaches organizations and businesses how to effectively apply Guerrilla Marketing principles. As a master certified coach, Kelvin's coaching work has impacted the lives of more than 20,000 people. In addition, Kelvin is the founder of Executive Coach International, a leading coaching organization whose campaigns have been featured in Asia's media – for instance, the publication of "Pick Me Up" - a collection of stories that was written and compiled into a book within 24 hours. Kelvin sits on the Board of Directors of New York City's political and social arts organization, The Culture Project, as well as participates in humanitarian activities at the United Nations.

GUERRILLA FACEBOOK MARKETING GLOSSARY

Apps are application software programmed to carry out a single or multiple tasks. On Facebook, apps are developed in-house as well as by a host of third-party developers for many purposes, from documentation to simulation to entertainment.

Analytics is a term to describe logical, in-depth monitoring and analysis of data and statistics by combining computer software technologies and methodologies in operational research. Analytics can monitor behaviour and trends, and make sophisticated correlations with static variables such as demographics. On Facebook, the end results are typically represented in visuals such as graphs in Facebook Insights.

Baseline comparison is a comparative data analysis method of evaluating variables against a pre-determined reference point.

Bounce Rate is a commonly-used term by Internet marketers in website traffic analysis to describe the percentage of unique visitors who only view a single page of a website and leave the site. A website with a low bounce rate suggests that the website has engaging content as visitors are spending time viewing more pages on that website. Bounce rates can help website developers assess the effectiveness of their landing page. See entry on Landing Page.

Click-through rate (CTR%) is a unit of measurement in web-based advertising to determine how effective an ad is, based on the action taken by the viewer (i.e. clicking on the ad). It is calculated by dividing the number of times the ad was shown by the number of clicks it received, expressed by a percentage. The higher the CTR%, the more effective the ad is deemed to be.

Cost per click (CPC) is a measurement in advertising based on what it cost for every click per advertisement. It is calculated by dividing the total cost for the ad by the total number of clicks on that ad. On Facebook, each click on an ad directs the visitor to the advertiser's page. Advertisements on Facebook are bid-based. See Cost per mille (CPM).

Cost per mille (CPM) or cost per thousand is a measurement in advertising based on what it cost for every thousand impressions (or views) of an advertisement. The word "mille" derives its meaning, "thousand" from French. The average CPM is calculated by dividing the cost of the ad by the number of thousands of times the advertisement is displayed. On Facebook, advertisers can set maximum amounts on daily advertising expenses. See Cost per click (CPC).

Dashboard is a term used in Facebook Insights that refers to the control panel from which users can view data (metrics) about their Facebook Page in various forms.

Fusion Marketing involves combining or tying in of one's marketing efforts with another partner for mutual profitability and maximum exposure. Guerrillas are dependent on their fusion marketing partners. For example, a local bakery could mention its neighbour's new store opening in their brochures and vice-versa. They know that the outcome of their marketing campaigns is strengthened by finding and working with their fusion partners.

Facebook Fan is a Facebook user who has chosen to be identified with or show support to a particular fan Page. There is no limit to the number of Pages a Facebook user can decide to be a fan of. Updates on the fan Page appears in the News Feed of the fan that can be viewed in turn by the fan's friends.

Facebook "Like" is a signature feature of Facebook that permits Facebook users an easy way to indicate their response by simply clicking on the word (or button) "Like". The mechanism behind Facebook's "Like" is extremely powerful as a means of word of mouth marketing. When a user "Likes" a comment or update or link, the information is shared through that user's friends on their News Feeds, which is turned can be viewed by friends of friends and so on.

Guerrilla Facebook Marketing weapons refer to Facebook-specific features, tools and resources that guerrillas can use to further their marketing plans. See Chapter 4 for 25 Facebook-specific weapons.

Landing Page is the first page that a visitor is directed to on Facebook, usually by clicking on a link or by typing in the address of the Page.

Marketing budget is a sum of money that is set aside to cover marketing expenses. For example, cost of advertisements. Guerrillas express their marketing budget as a percentage of their gross sales, before deductibles.

Marketing Calendar is a chronological sequencing of a marketing plan expressed in a calendar format - hourly/daily/weekly/monthly/yearly. It goes hand-in-hand with a marketing plan. See Marketing Plan.

Marketing Plan is a set of intended actions through which one executes to achieve a goal or goals. A guerrilla's marketing plan consists of 7 elements and is succinctly expressed in 7 sentences. See Chapter 5 on Commence Battle Plan. A marketing plan can be complemented with a marketing calendar. See Marketing Calendar in Chapter 5.

Market survey can be defined as an attempt to collect information about consumers or markets to support or help make marketing decisions. Information can be collected through a variety of research techniques, such as opinion research or statistical analysis. Typical market surveys include analysing consumer behaviour, what consumer wants, and demand and supply of different commodities.

Mashups in techno-terms refers to a web application that combines or integrates multiple and complementary functions into something new. Google Maps, for instance, has mashups with numerous providers to offer users new functions. See for example, locating public toilets anywhere in the world (www.safe2pee.org). Sometimes also spelt as mash-ups. Similar to, but not the same as Fusion Marketing. See separate entry.

Moderator is a person in web-based forums or discussions authorized to enforce rules or guidelines of the forum. Moderators are granted access to all discussions threads and posts, and they can typically answer, delete, move, remove and block posts or users who do not comply with the guidelines of the forum or discussion.

Open source The concept of free sharing, accessibility, use and modification of content or software by the public. Web browser Mozilla Firefox and office software Open Office are examples of open sourced software. Wikipedia is an example of an open-source content that anyone can modify.

Poll is a survey conducted to determine public opinion by means of voting. Guerrilla Facebook Marketers can employ polls as a means of gathering opinion as well as engaging fans. On Facebook, users can conduct polls by means of the Facebook Question function, or by using a poll app.

Positioning is a term in marketing that refers to your niche in the marketplace – what your brands stands for. It is one of the 7 elements in a Guerrilla's marketing plan. See Chapter 5 on Commence Battle Plan.

Privacy setting permits Facebook users control by limiting the sharing of content and data sharing. In recent times, Facebook has introduced more ways that permit users more sophisticated ways to control the nature of content shared with selected groups of friends.

Prospects are defined as potential customers identified by marketers.

ROI (Return on Investment) is a ratio of money gained or lost in relation to the amount of money invested and expressed as a percentage. For guerrillas, ROI is always measured in terms of profits.

Social bookmarking refers to the sharing of Internet links and references by visitors on websites such as Digg.com and del.icio.us.

Social graph is the global mapping of people and how they are related to one another. It suggests the future direction of the World Wide Web, with many implications for service providers, social media and web developers. The term is believed to have been introduced by Facebook in a 2007 Facebook convention under the concept of Facebook Platform.

Social Media refers to the use of media for social interaction - communicate, connect, buy, recommend, share, review, network, and so on. Facebook and Twitter are examples of social media.

Syndication feeds permit summaries of content on one website to be made available on another website for greater web exposure. RSS Graffiti and Blog RSS are examples of syndication feeds in Facebook.

Target Market refers to a specific segment that a marketer identifies to focus his/her marketing efforts on. Guerrillas carve out specific target markets by establishing geographic (by location, city or country), demographic (gender, age) and/or psychographic factors (similar interests, spending habits, etc).

Unique Selling Proposition (USP) is a marketing concept that focuses on highlighting the benefit(s) that can only be provided by a particular business. Also known as Unique Selling Point.

Unique visitor is a statistical variable commonly used in analytics to refer to a visitor to a website who has never visited before within a specified time period. The higher the number of unique visitors to a website, the more effective the marketing campaign has been in garnering new prospects.

User Generated Content (UGC) is a new concept that refers to content created not only by website owners but also by users and visitors. Genres that have arisen from UGC include fan-fiction, customer review sites, discussion boards, trip planners, wikis, and so on.

Viral Marketing is the replication or spreading of marketing messages, usually in an expedient manner similar to that of how a virus is spread – via word of mouth, or by text messages, or via social networking sites such as Facebook or Twitter.

Web traffic refers to data collected on the web. Specifically, website owners and marketers focus on web traffic data such as the number of visitors to their websites as an indicator of the website's popularity. Web traffic can be directed from one website to another by enticing users to click on ads or links, by search engines, via emails and so on.

Wikis are online knowledge databases of collaborated content created by permitting the public to contribute content by editing, adding, deleting and sharing new content. Wikipedia is the largest online encyclopedia, but wiki applications have extended to the creation of FAQs, note-taking, and even to teaching instructions. See for example, Meatball Wiki.

GUERRILLA MARKETING RESOURCES

www.gmarketing.com

*Official Guerrilla Marketing Website
by Jay Levinson*

Highlights:
Introduction to Guerrilla Marketing, an interactive marketing
support system designed for business owners

www.guerrillamarketing.asia

*Official Guerrilla Marketing Consulting Website
by Kelvin Lim*

Highlights:
Introduction to Guerrilla Marketing Consulting services,
including Guerrilla Marketing Training Program, a program
designed to teach business owners to be
successful Guerrillas based in Asia
See you on Facebook

www.facebook.com/learnguerrillamarketing

Like Us on Facebook and be in touch with other guerrillas
and be keep in the loop for events and meet-ups

CPSIA information can be obtained at www.ICGtesting.com
Printed in the USA
LVOW131707060313

323026LV00007B/688/P